COMICS
for
CHOICE

SECOND EDITION

We first published *Comics for Choice* soon after Trump was elected, and the future of abortion access in the United States looked perilous. We wanted to inform readers about the history of abortion rights, the diverse reasons people get abortions, and the many barriers we need to tear down to get to real reproductive freedom. Denying abortion care is a dangerous, monstrous injustice.

Now that the Supreme Court has overturned *Roe v Wade*, which protected the Constitutional right to abortion in the U.S. for almost fifty years, over half of U.S. states have made abortion illegal or highly restricted. In those states, losing a pregnancy could be investigated as a crime, with all the modern tools of digital surveillance. Fetal personhood laws have the potential to be even more oppressive, criminalizing anything that could be considered harmful to a fetus.

Even when *Roe* stood, actual access to abortion was extremely varied and often impossible. Clinics have been forced to close for decades due to targeted legal restrictions and terrorist attacks. Traveling to a faraway clinic takes time and money that many can ill-afford, especially if they're parents already. Abortion care itself is often expensive. We were proud to raise money for the National Network of Abortion Funds with the first edition of this book, and supporting abortion funds remains one of the most important ways to give people agency over their pregnancies, and thus, their lives.

Information on accessing and using abortion pills for self-directed care has become even more critical to mitigating the harmful impact of bans. Since the first edition, options for telemedicine abortion have expanded dramatically, and alternate routes of access to abortion pills are now a reality in all 50 states via online pharmacies and human rights organizations, even where politicians are blocking access to care.

My hope lies in the activists and organizations who have decades of experience overcoming obstacles to abortion care and have been anticipating the fall of *Roe v Wade*, as well as a generation of Americans who have always understood abortion as a fundamental right. We need to protect every person's access to abortion and remove barriers to healthcare of all kinds.

Hazel Newlevant, Co-Editor

When Hazel proposed the idea of co-editing an anthology about abortion with Ø.K. Fox following the election of Trump in 2016, I gladly jumped at the opportunity. Around that time, a few years out of my Master of Public Health (MPH) program, I was working as a clinical health educator in NYC, teaching sex ed and providing reproductive health services, including birth control and pregnancy "options" counseling. This experience opened my eyes to the diversity of experiences, values, and beliefs that people hold around a variety of topics, including abortion. As a cartoonist, I have always cherished storytelling and how comics have the power to relay personal, educational, and journalistic narratives in a clear and compelling way. At the time, I knew that the comics medium would be an impactful choice for challenging pre-conceived notions, increasing knowledge, and tackling stigma around abortion.

Years later, I feel this even stronger, with the Supreme Court's overturning of *Roe*, a precedent that many of us younger citizens have never lived without. With abortion laws left up to individual states, we will increasingly live in a country with a hodgepodge of rules, restrictions, and resources most impacting the vulnerable.

In the past few years, I've also become a mother by choice. I've become more aware of the maternal mortality crisis affecting women, particularly women of color, in the US. I've experienced how the COVID-19 pandemic has further weakened the already limited childcare infrastructure and social safety net that make parenting affordable, safe, and manageable. Having a pregnant body and being a caregiver has made me more aware of what is at stake if abortion rights and services continue to be threatened in the US.

That is why we must continue to speak, write, and draw our stories.

Whit Taylor, Co-Editor

As a certified trans-guy-abortion-haver I was proud to be involved with the first edition of this project and share a little of my struggles in our deeply corrupt, shabby excuse for a medical system. I have since come to understand myself as one of countless medicalized bodies in the surplus population the ruling class has deemed fit to cull in its system of cruelty. Many had a similar awakening during the pandemic. Uterus or not, our struggles are linked in the fight against our coerced, rigidly imposed positions in life. We deserve choice—more than the choice to have an abortion, the people should no longer be denied their clear choice for Medicare for all or single payer healthcare. This is a choice the people have clearly made within the labyrinthian boundaries of the United States electoral process countless times. Now the stakes are higher, and we cannot continue to accept capitalist expansion, despite the material benefits we may have as subjects of Western empire. Those benefits are a farce—there is a far more prosperous collective liberation to be won.

Beyond the nonprofit industrial complex, we must keep building new working class institutions, like the heartening amount of mutual aid networks formed in the past couple of years, to both protect and enact our choices. The time and resources we've already dedicated to this work has been strenuous, but continuing to organize and formalize our formations will increase efficiency and international support. We stand in solidarity with every politicized population facing abortion criminalization, denial of care, and the general lowering of life expectancies.

My eternal revolutionary love to you,

Ø.K. Fox, Co-Editor

Further reading:
"We Are Not Crumbs, We Must Not Accept Crumbs" speech by Larry Kramer
Health Communism by Beatrice Adler-Bolton and

Mutual Aid: Building Solidarity During This Crisis (and the Next) by Dean Spade
The Faggots & Their Friends Between Revolutions

Table of Contents

Mission Abolition: against Adoption and Abortion Bans

Lizartistry and Leah Nichols

PRESS START

It was Year 2022. The year the U.S. Supreme Court overturned Roe.

"Don't Abort, Adopt!" had long been a battle-cry used by **Anti-Abortion** agents in their war on **Bodily Autonomy**. In 2022, they shouted it more loudly and violently than ever, flanked by unknowing accomplices who never thought to question their **beliefs and assumptions** about Adoption.

But many **Adopted People** fought back, wielding their own experiences and voices against the suffocating smoke of disinformation.

Earth's atmosphere was explosive.

Adoption is a choice.

Abortion is a decision about whether to give birth or not. Adoption is a decision about whether to parent a child or not. They are not equivalents.

Adopted people don't have abortions.

My mother wanted to raise me but didn't have the resources. She felt she didn't have a choice. #AdopteesForChoice

I was adopted and I have had an abortion!

Adopted people are and should be grateful.

Adoption is an act of love.

The practice of adoption cannot be separated from the adoption industry, which is built on regulation, control, and the accumulation of profit.

Adopted people do not owe gratitude to the people that made decisions about our lives when we were unable or unallowed to.

In the universe you are about to enter, the world has cracked open and a clusterfuck of crises is exploding into the void of space.

Battling **Abortion Bans** and **Adoption**, workers for **Autonomy** and **Self-Determined Kinship** seek to build a community to fight back.

Will you join the community?
Press A to begin.

ABORTION BANS

ADOPTION

Hello, Player! Congratulations on your first mission! Let's see what intelligence you have gathered about Abortion Bans and Adoption.

"Adopt, Don't Abort!"

This card can gains Legibility through appeals to White Supremacy and Ableism.

This card cannot function unless Nulear Family is already in play on the field.

Adoption Industry

Adoption Industry boasts the following abilities: Family Separation, Veneer of Benevolence, and Closed Records.

This card is part of the Billion Dollar Industry expansion set, along with Prison Industrial Complex and Transnational Corporations.

Family Regulation

If Family Regulation is in your hand, you have the abilities of Policing, Surveillance, and Family Separation.

This card inflicts 10x damage when played against certain opponents. See the White Supremacist, Capitalist, Ableist Playbook for more.

Great job, Player! It looks like these cards can be played by both liberals and conservatives. But no fear! Bodily Autonomy and Self-Determined Kinship have been building their own arsenal of liberatory strategies and dreams.

"Your Body, Your Choice!"

When this card is on the field, any cards that restrict Bodily Autonomy are removed from play.

This card deals 20 damage any time a player has an Abortion or gains Access to Birth Records.

Self-Determination of Children

This card delivers direct damage to Commodification of Children.

This card also strips any Pro-Life or Pro-Choice cards on the field of their defensive abilities by exposing the false narrative of "best interests of the child."

Queering Kinship

This card creates stronger relationships amongst cards in play that support Self-Determination and Connection.

When this card is in play, all cards associated with Heteronormativity and Nuclear Family automatically are removed from the field.

Well done! You have obtained your first three cards. Before you go, check out the Resources below to set you forth in the right direction!

How All Politics Became Reproductive Politics: From Welfare Reform to Foreclosure to Trump by Laura Briggs

The Child Catchers: Rescue, Trafficking, and the New Gospel of Adoption by Kathryn Joyce

Torn Apart: How the Child Welfare System Destroys Black Families — and How Abolition Can Build a Safer World by Dorothy Roberts

Okay, Emma. Let's just get through this day. Everything is going to be fine.

bzz—

Be right out!

GOD HATES ABORTION

BABY KILLER

It's going to be okay.

A COUPLE HOURS LATER...

ENCOUNTERING ABORTION RESTRICTIONS, FROM KENYA TO TEXAS

STORY BY: MJ FLORES   ART BY: KAT FAJARDO

My name is MJ Flores.
I was born and raised in Texas
as a child of immigrants –
Latino and Middle Eastern.

I was fortunate to attend
Harvard for college,
have worked in international
development to help provide
others with the same
opportunities as I have,
and am a social impact
strategy consultant here
in beautiful DC.

I'm a fan of hot Texas summers,
grew up eating tacos and kabobs,
and my favorite singer will
forever be Selena.

I've also had
an abortion.

After college, I chose to work in rural Kenya to help coordinate health and education programs.

I was dating a guy at the time, and my birth control failed. Multiple forms of birth control failed – the condom broke, the morning after pill did not work.

I never thought I would ever experience an unplanned pregnancy – most of us never do – and, despite being supportive of abortion access, I never imagined I would get an abortion if I did get pregnant.

I was wrong.

I Googled some of my symptoms, assuming I was ill with something. Google was the first one to tell me I was pregnant.

Then, I saw the first pregnancy test turn positive. I was not ready to have a child, and I knew immediately what I was going to do – I was going to get an abortion.

Out of shock, I took two more pregnancy tests and then traveled three hours to the nearby town to get an ultrasound because I could not believe this was happening to me.

I burst out into tears when I saw the ultrasound. The doctor tried to shush me, and asked a female nurse to come in and take care of me.

She told me it would be okay, it would work out.

I responded: but I thought abortion was illegal in Kenya.

She chastised me for even thinking about an abortion, just as those who protest outside clinics do. But that did not dissuade me.

Because abortion is largely illegal in Kenya, I decided I was going to get an abortion back in my home state, Texas.

While I couldn't afford the flight back, I was lucky. My employer was already planning to move me back to the US. I waited two long weeks before I could get on that flight.

In the meantime, I hid the news from the people around me in this small rural town where everyone knew everything. People just thought I was sick. I called Planned Parenthood back in the U.S. when I could, late at night in Kenya in my bedroom.

I tried to get as much information as possible to understand my options, and scheduled an appointment. The day arrived and I was on that plane.

But I wasn't off the hook yet. Texas also had its own restrictive anti-abortion laws that I had to fulfill... during a layover in the London airport.

The thing is that I was going to land in Texas with probably just one day left to get a medical abortion (my chosen procedure) as permitted under state law. But – Texas also had a one-day waiting period requirement.

So, in order to make it in on time, I found a corner in the airport during my layover in London, sat down, and called a doctor thousands of miles away just so the clock would start ticking on the waiting period.

Although abortion is a safe and common procedure, the doctor was mandated by the state to read me lies about made-up and long-disproven risks and complications.

I was afraid the travelers around me would hear my conversation, but I should never have had to go through that.

I knew my decision and didn't need to listen to lies or undergo a day-long waiting period in what was already an emotionally and physically exhausting situation.

Planned Parenthood

I finally landed in Texas and went to Planned Parenthood where I had my abortion – I made it in time.

The provider in Planned Parenthood was great, and the clinic provided me with a needed subsidy – they ensured that the low salary I was making in Kenya was not going to keep me from my right to choose.

I took the first pills of the regimen at the clinic, and the second set at home.

I received supportive and honest care, unlike what legislators in Texas had given me with their unnecessary and patronizing laws.

Anti-choice laws made it difficult for me to access my safe and legal abortion. And I had assumed that my difficulties were going to stop once I was able to overcome these barriers.

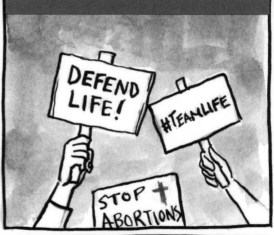

But I could not predict the heaviness of the stigma. I had never felt such loneliness in my life until the weeks and months that followed my abortion.

The stigma was silencing, and I did not tell anyone except for the handful of people closest to me, to whom I am still forever grateful.

All I wanted in those moments was to talk to someone who had had an abortion—and I knew no one.

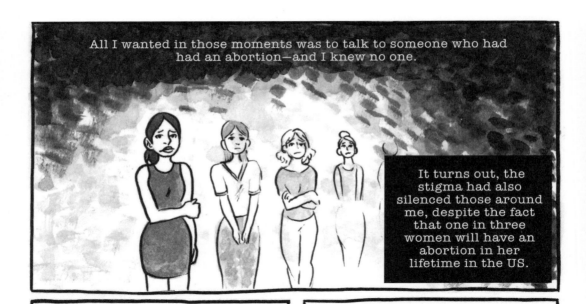

It turns out, the stigma had also silenced those around me, despite the fact that one in three women will have an abortion in her lifetime in the US.

And because I knew no one, because I felt that part of this country hated me with the anti-choice laws that were being passed throughout the country, I did not share my story for many years – and it was crushing.

Slowly, however, I started to tell my friends and family. I wanted to share this part of me with them.

And they responded...with love. So much love and empathy and affirmation that gave me the strength to overcome the stigma.

It was their words and hugs, their growing involvement to support reproductive rights, that has helped propel me to share my story publicly.

Before the first time I shared in a group, a friend asked me how many people I had told. I wrote all their names down. 100 people. I had told 100 people.

I was ready.

I shared my story publicly for the first time in front of a group of students, my friends, while I was in graduate school. I am so thankful to them.

Since then, I have shared my story in news outlets, in magazine interviews, even in front of 9,000 people where Sia performed and Lucy Flores spoke at the All Access Concert in Ohio.

Still, every time I hear about a new anti-choice law that's passed or an attack on Planned Parenthood which gave me the life I have right now, the life that is dedicated to others, I get nervous.

Because I go back to five years ago and I get nervous that I wouldn't be able to get an abortion, to make my own choice.

My body feels imprisoned, trapped, and I scream inside.

I know an unintended pregnancy can happen again, to me and to anyone else, and I am made worried by the onslaught of these attacks on our rights and our retrogression to that harder, more unforgiving, less understanding country we used to be...and as we still see in other parts of the world.

So I urge everyone, to remember that it can happen to them, or their sister, their wife, their friend, and speak up in support of abortion access to your friends and family,

sign the petitions,

call your Representatives,

and donate to clinics, abortion funds, and advocacy organizations if you can.

DONATE

If you are not ready to share your story or do not have a story to share, you now have mine.

Please share it – let's remind people that choices around abortion happen to real people who should have autonomy over their bodies and lives.

The stigma silenced me for too long. But I no longer will be silenced, and together, we can silence the stigma.

YOU ONLY KEEP ONE BULL

AN INTERVIEW WITH MY GRANDMOTHER
BY KENDRA JOSIE KIRKPATRICK

PREGNANCY WAS VERY SECRETIVE BEFORE THE PILL.

GIRLS WENT TO 'HOMES FOR UNWED MOTHERS'. THE FLORENCE CRITTENTON HOMES WERE THE MOST WELL KNOWN.

AN EXCUSE WOULD BE MADE TO EVERYONE...

I'M GOING TO VISIT MY GRANDMA A BIT... FOR

...AND THEN, THEY WOULD SHOW UP SEVERAL MONTHS LATER.

WELCOME BACK, HOW WAS YOUR GRANDMA?

HUH?? MY GRANDMA? I WASN'T WI-₹ OH! I MEAN...

AROUND WHEN THE PILL WAS POPULARIZED, I WAS BUSY HAVING MY KIDS.

I BEGAN WORKING IN THE WOMAN'S HEALTH CLINIC AT THE UNIVERSITY OF MARYLAND, IN THE BASEMENT.

SEXUAL HEALTH

S.T.D.S HOW TO STAY CLEAN

UNPLANNED PREGNANCY ? ? ?

TWO GIRLS COME TO MIND...

BUT I ONLY HAD SEX *ONCE*, HOW AM I PREGNANT?

LACK OF UNDERSTANDING WAS A PROBLEM.

WELL, I *HAVE* A DIAPHAGM IN MY ROOM, BUT I LEFT IT IN MY DRAWER . . .

THERE WAS A CATHOLIC PRIEST WHO WAS SECRETLY CONNECTED TO THE CLINIC.

HE WOULD PARDON THE CATHOLIC GIRLS CONSIDERING ABORTION.

I'M PRO-CHOICE PARTLY BECAUSE OF WORKING IN THAT CLINIC. PEOPLE ARE YOUNG, AND MAKE MISTAKES.

WOMEN HAVE *ALWAYS* HAD ABORTIONS, THEY WERE JUST BACK ALLEY.

THE WHOLE POINT OF ROE VS. WADE WAS TO GUARANTEE ONE THING...

...ABORTIONS WOULD BE PERFORMED IN A SAFE ENVIROMENT.

WHILE RAISING MY KIDS, I WASN'T THAT AWARE OF THE INCREASING VIOLENCE AGAINST ABORTION CLINICS...

THESE EXTREMISTS CALL THEMSELVES "CHRISTIANS."

THEY THINK IT'S OK TO KILL DOCTORS IN ORDER TO "SAVE" UNBORN "BABIES."

ONCE MY KIDS GREW UP, I GOT MORE INVOLVED.

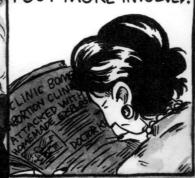

LAST YEAR, I PUT A NEW BUMPER STICKER ON MY CAR.

PRO CHILD PRO CHOICE

ONE DAY, I NOTICED A WOMAN FOLLOWING ME IN HER CAR...

HOW CAN YOU BE "PRO-CHILD" AND PRO-CHOICE?!

WHEN I PULLED INTO THE GAS STATION, THE WOMAN SHOUTED...

WELL—

I'D HAVE LOVED TO DISCUSS IT WITH HER, BUT SHE DROVE OFF.

PEOPLE DON'T THINK, THEY REACT.

TO THE MEN WHO THINK WOMEN'S BODIES SHOULD BE USED ONLY FOR PROPAGATING THE SPECIES...

...I LIKE TO POINT OUT THAT IF YOU'RE RAISING CATTLE, ALL THESE MEN WHO THINK THEIR OPINION IS MORE IMPORTANT THEN A WOMAN'S CHOICE...

...THEY'D ALL BE IRRELEVANT...

...BECAUSE YOU ONLY KEEP ONE BULL AROUND.

INSERT **KNITTING NEEDLE** IN UTERUS

DRINK DETERGENT

SUDSO

BEAT STOMACH WITH **BASEBALL BAT**

SPEND THE NIGHT IN THE SNOW

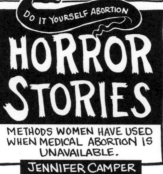

DO IT YOURSELF ABORTION

HORROR STORIES

METHODS WOMEN HAVE USED WHEN MEDICAL ABORTION IS UNAVAILABLE.

JENNIFER CAMPER

SQUIRT SOAP AND TURPENTINE IN UTERUS

SOAP

TURP

DRINK **BLEACH**

BLEACH

INSERT CHILI PEPPERS IN **VAGINA**

FALL DOWN STAIRS

INSERT A BICYCLE SPOKE IN UTERUS

INSERT A **COAT HANGER** INTO UTERUS

DRINK **LYE**

LYE

TAKE A BATH IN **BOILING WATER**

STARVE

FALL OFF ROOF

They Called Her Dr. D:

Tennessee's first
Black woman legislator
and abortion reform

Writer: Dr. Cynthia Greenlee
Artist: Jaz Malone

Dorothy Brown
Born: c. 1919
Died: 2004

Just an infant, Dorothy Brown was placed in a New York orphanage.

Her mother couldn't take care of her.

Being born an orphan led her to develop the idea that –

– if you don't want to have a baby, you shouldn't have to.

At age five, she got her tonsils out, and decided then and there she wanted to be a doctor.

She worked as a maid to support herself,
until she won a scholarship
to Bennett College in North Carolina.

She hit the books,
and won admission
to medical school.

She was the only woman in a sea of male residents...

...and became the first female surgeon from Merharry, a Black medical school in Tennessee.

Some of the fellows called me "Mule Brown" because I worked so hard. I never let anything bother me.

Known as "Dr. D," she operated on women who came to the hospital with injuries from abortions, which were illegal.

They call me "The Lady Who Cuts."

Finally, someone asked her if she wanted to run for state office, as a representative in the Tennessee legistlature.

She did, and won.

Another first:
First Black woman legislator in the Senate.

Before abortion was legalized in Roe v. Wade, she had provided abortions.

I don't think I broke the law. What was in the book of statutes was that a woman could have a termination if it would spare the mother.

She would run from the Capitol to the hospital to see patients. And finally, she decided to –

- do something for my profession.

Bill No. 931

In 1967, she introduced a bill to change the state's abortion law, which only allowed women to have abortions if they were going to die from the pregnancy.

The bill proposed allowing abortion in cases of rape and incest.

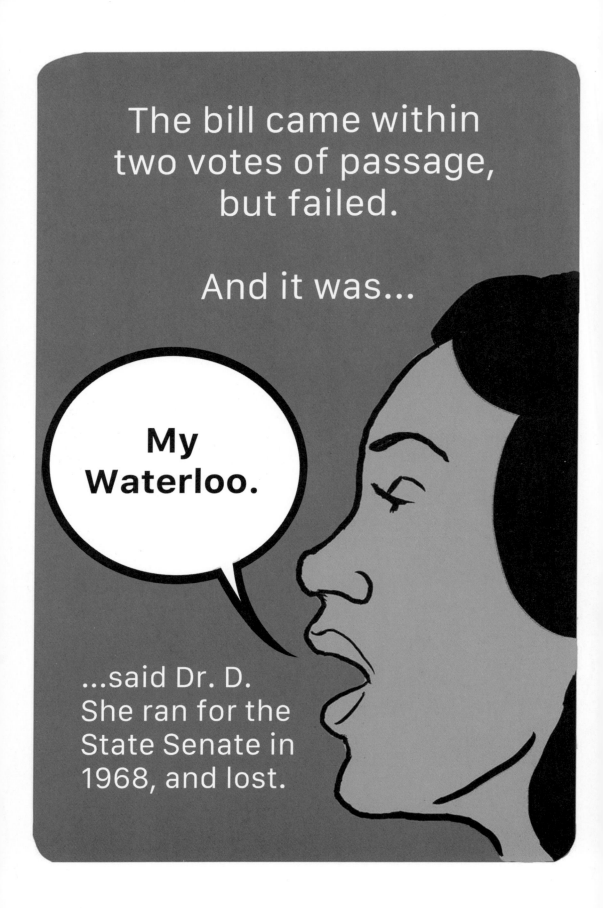

Dr. D kept on moving.

Throughout her political and medical careers, she:

 Lobbied for "Negro History Month"

 Established a human relations commission

 Became one of the first single women
to adopt in her state

 Battled the idea that abortion was an anti-Black
racial conspiracy

In 1973, she told a
health conference:

Now first, let's
dispense with 'genocide'!

There's been genocide
in this country
since 1619.

Dorothy Brown always
said what she meant
and meant what she said.

THE END

ABORTION TRIALS

Story by Rickie Solinger   Art by Rachel Merrill

Transcripts of pre-Roe v. Wade abortion trials are scary to read.
And not because they tell grisly tales about back-alley butchers and death.
Public health records show far fewer incompetent practitioners than
popular history has claimed. The trials make such difficult reading
because they show how in St. Louis, Los Angeles, Sacramento, Trenton,
New York — all over the country — girls and women were pulled into
courtrooms to testify not about their decisions to murder their own
unborn child, but about how they had the temerity to murder motherhood,
the only true destiny for real women.

President Donald J. Trump promised to send the matter of abortion
"back to the states" and to appoint judges and Supreme Court
justices who would oversee the process. Indeed, after the death
of Justice Ruth Bader Ginsburg, Trump appointed his third justice,
giving the Supreme Court a robust anti-abortion majority dedicated
to overturning Roe v. Wade, in June 2022. Many states did
criminalize abortion. This left untold numbers of unwillingly or
unsafely pregnant individuals to try to terminate their
pregnancies, no matter what the law says — as such people have
always done. When criminal abortion trials were at their peak
after World War II, public health experts estimated one million
illegal procedures were performed every year in the U.S. Now that
states are recriminalizing abortion, there will, once again, be
abortions, arrests, trials, and convictions.

As frightening as it was to sneak off for an illegal abortion in the decades preceding Roe, before feminists had defined reproductive health as a human right, the courtroom could be even more frightening, even a house of horrors. Attorneys defending the practitioner aimed to undermine the credibility of the prosecution's witnesses by describing girls and women who terminated their pregnancies as immoral, dishonest and willing to do anything for their own welfare. The typical girl, one lawyer said in court, tells her boyfriend that she needs $250 or $500 and then she goes off to buy some pretty new clothes. How, he asked the jury, can you take the testimony of that kind of girl against my client? A popular defense tactic was to get the girl to admit that she had slept with a man not her husband,or that she was just plain promiscuous. The lawyer for the defense asked one young woman if she had been pregnant before, and if she were, indeed, not married, and how many men she had had sex with, all questions that the judge forced responses to.

**Prosecutors called for making pregnancy "reportable,"
and for bringing criminal charges against girls and
women who terminated their pregnancies.**

Quite often, prosecuting lawyers seemed to act on the
theory that the more sexual references and sexual innuendo
they could spread around in the courtroom, the more perverse
the case and the more perverted and culpable the accused.

Over and over in these trials, women were forced to
describe how they undressed in the practitioner's office.
They were forced to describe
whether and how the practitioner
put a hand or a finger into
their private parts.
In many of these postwar
trials, girls and women had
pictures of their bodies
drawn on courtroom chalkboards
for the edification of
the audience. They sat
in the witness box as
the abortion table was
wheeled into the
courtroom and placed in
front of them.

The trial transcripts and the newspaper coverage of the trials show that the lawyers and the judges running these trials, along with the journalists covering them and the doctors and others who testified, and even the interested citizens who filled up the courtrooms, did not seem to find the eroticization of the court inappropriate or unseemly.

In the public courtroom, women were thoroughly degraded and humiliated, the most private facts of their lives publicly revealed and reviled: their bodies, their sexuality, their wombs, the intimate sources of their personal dignity. The doctors, lawyers, judges, journalist, and myriad expert witnesses spoke up, one by one, to reaffirm their prerogatives over women's bodies and their lives. And their leverage extended beyond the courtroom because the displays in the morning papers after an abortion raid and the theatrics in the courtrooms carried powerful cultural messages.

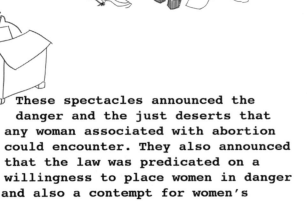

These spectacles announced the danger and the just deserts that any woman associated with abortion could encounter. They also announced that the law was predicated on a willingness to place women in danger and also a contempt for women's self-determination.

Anyone could see that enforcing anti-abortion laws involved the degradation of women. In this way, the mid-twentieth-century prosecution of women associated with abortion embodied the message that every woman, whether or not she ever had or ever would climb up on the abortion table, was endangered by the statutes that criminalized abortion.

Now that the Supreme Court has allowed—encouraged—the recriminalization of abortion by state legislatures, vast numbers of pregnant people will see their claims for full citizenship status and human rights endangered and denied, depending on the state where they live.

JANE

RACHEL WILSON
ALLY SHWED

SINCE THE LATE 1970's, JUDITH ARCANA HAS WORKED WITH AND SPOKEN TO HUNDREDS OF WOMEN ON ANYTHING FROM FEMINISM TO TATTOOING...

...BUT WHATEVER THE TOPIC, THERE'S ALWAYS ONE QUESTION SHE GETS ASKED REPEATEDLY.

Do you think, um...

I was just wondering...

How do you manage to set up an illegal abortion service?

THIS IS BECAUSE, BETWEEN 1969 AND 1973, JUDITH AND OVER A HUNDRED OTHER WOMEN HELPED PROVIDE ACCESS TO ILLEGAL ABORTION SERVICES

OPERATING UNDER THE CODE NAME:

JANE

CHICAGO WOMEN'S ABORTION RIGHTS

OFFICIALLY KNOWN AS THE ABORTION COUNSELING SERVICE OF THE CHICAGO WOMEN'S LIBERATION UNION, JANE BEGAN SIMPLY AS A REFERRAL SERVICE.

There's a doctor we can get you in touch with.

BUT SOON IT BECAME A FEMINIST GROUP IN WHICH MEMBERS LEARNED TO PERFORM THE ABORTIONS THEMSELVES.

THEY WOULD PERFORM AN ESTIMATED 11,000 IN TOTAL BEFORE THEY FOLDED IN 1973, THE YEAR ROE V. WADE MADE ABORTION LEGAL IN ALL OF AMERICA.

SOON, HEATHER RECEIVED MORE AND MORE **CALLS.**

ILLEGAL ABORTION WASN'T DISCUSSED OPENLY, ONLY HEARD ABOUT WHEN A WOMAN TURNED UP DEAD. BUT WITH A GROWING NUMBER OF WOMEN SEEKING HELP, HEATHER REALIZED ABORTION WASN'T A MEDICAL ISSUE — IT WAS A **FEMINIST** ONE.

THEY CHOSE <u>JANE</u>.

THE JANES WERE UNHAPPY WITH HOW **LITTLE CONTROL** THEY HAD OVER THE PROCESS. ABORTIONISTS CHARGED BETWEEN

$500 *to* $1000

AND WOULDN'T ALLOW WOMEN TO BE **ACCOMPANIED**. ALL THE JANES COULD DO WAS CHECK ON THEM <u>AFTER</u> THE PROCEDURE.

THUS, THE GROUP WAS ABLE TO REGULATE THE PROCESS FROM *start* TO *finish*, KNOWING WOMEN WOULD BE **SAFE** IN THEIR HANDS AND SUPPORTED <u>ALL</u> THE WAY THROUGH.

HAVING ATTAINED **AUTONOMY**, THE GROUP REFINED ITS PROTOCOL.

CALL-BACK JANE

ANSWERING MACHINE

Hi, this is Jane. We got your message. I'm calling back to get your basic medical history...

Don't worry.

I'm going to explain the process to you, then we'll go ahead and set up your appointment, okay?

COUNSELOR

WOMEN WOULD COME TO **THE FRONT**, AN APARTMENT DONATED TO THE JANES AS A KIND OF WAITING ROOM.

BEFORE BEING DRIVEN TO **THE PLACE**, WHERE JANE ABORTION PROVIDERS PERFORMED PROCEDURES ALL DAY.

I'll tell you about the painkillers on the ride home.

THE COUNSELORS WOULD THEN FOLLOW UP WITH EACH WOMAN IN THE DAYS AFTER HER PROCEDURE TO ENSURE THAT NO COMPLICATIONS HAD ARISEN.

SINCE THEY WORKED IN THE DAYS **BEFORE "MEDICAL" ABORTIONS**—THOSE INDUCED BY THE **MIFEPRISTONE-MISOPROSTOL**—ALL JANE ABORTIONS WERE **SURGICAL**.

RU-486

JANE PROVIDERS WOULD USE THE **DILATION** AND **CURETTAGE** METHOD; THIS INVOLVED DILATING THE CERVIX, ADMINISTERING LOCAL ANESTHETIC AND THEN SCRAPING FETAL TISSUE FROM THE UTERINE WALLS.

THIS METHOD WAS ONLY SUITABLE FOR EARLY TERM PREGNANCIES OF UP TO 12 WEEKS. FOR LONGER TERM CASES, A **MISCARRIAGE** HAD TO BE INDUCED. THIS WAS MORE EMOTIONALLY CHALLENGING, BUT JANE BELIEVED IN A

WOMAN'S ABSOLUTE **AUTHORITY** OVER HER OWN BODY.

WHEN THE WOMEN OF JANE PICKED UP THEIR INSTRUMENTS AND PERFORMED ABORTIONS, A WOMAN'S **RIGHT TO CHOOSE** QUITE LITERALLY BECAME PALPABLE *in their hands.*

IT'S A DIZZYING AND EMPOWERING THOUGHT, BUT FORMER JANES REMEMBER BEING UNDAUNTED BY THE PROSPECT.

JEANNE GALATZER-LEVY

JOINED JANE AFTER DROPPING OUT OF COLLEGE

It was the confidence of youth!

I was an idiot! I was 20 years old and it didn't scare me at all! One of the most radical things to come out of the women's movement was the change in medical culture. It was so PATERNALISTIC.

How dare you even look at yourself or think about your own body! In the process of breaking with that, who knew where the boundaries should be?

JANES ENCOURAGED THEIR COUNSELEES TO LOOK ON THE PROCESS AS **COLLABORATIVE** AND **EDUCATIVE**. WOMEN CAME *through* THE SERVICE, NOT *to* IT. NEITHER WERE THE WOMEN REFERRED TO AS *patients* OR *clients*, IN ORDER NOT TO REPLICATE THE MEDICAL AND **CAPITALIST CULTURE** THESE WORDS IMPLIED.

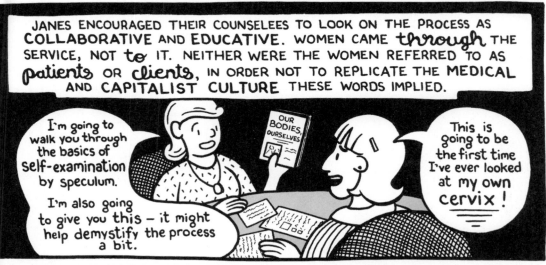

I'm going to walk you through the basics of self-examination by speculum.

I'm also going to give you this — it might help demystify the process a bit.

OUR BODIES, OURSELVES

This is going to be the first time I've ever looked at my own cervix!

BY CUTTING OUT THE ILLEGAL ABORTIONISTS THEY PREVIOUSLY RELIED ON, THE JANES WERE ABLE TO LOWER THE PRICE OF ABORTIONS TO JUST $100 —

I could only get $15... is that enough?

Absolutely. Thank you.

— BUT THEY **NEVER** TURNED AWAY A WOMAN WHO COULD PAY **NOTHING AT ALL.**

We figured if we averaged $50, we could make our expenses.

FINANCIAL CONTRIBUTIONS WERE SEEN AS ANOTHER WAY FOR WOMEN TO BECOME *active* PARTICIPANTS IN THEIR CHOICES, AS ANY PAYMENT MADE HELPED OTHER WOMEN TO ACCESS REPRODUCTIVE RIGHTS.

RECOGNIZING THAT AMERICA RAN ON WOMEN'S UNPAID LABOR — AND AS THEIR WORK WAS OF VALUE — JANES ALSO BEGAN TO PAY THEIR OWN MEMBERS.

GIVEN THE RELATIVELY LOW COST OF A JANE ABORTION, THE FRONT BECAME A **RARE POINT OF DIVERSITY** IN THE OTHERWISE WHITE, MIDDLE-CLASS LANDSCAPE OF WOMEN'S LIBERATION.

ANY WOMAN CAN BECOME PREGNANT WHO DOESN'T REALLY WANT TO BE. THERE WAS JUST AN ENORMOUS RESPECT FOR EVERYONE. —JEANNE GALATZER-LEVY

THERE WERE ONLY A FEW **WOMEN OF COLOR** IN JANE'S MEMBERSHIP AT ANY ONE TIME, AND **LOIS SMITH*** WAS ONE. IN AN INTERVIEW WITH LORETTA J. ROSS, SHE REMEMBERS: "WE COULD NEVER DEVELOP A CRITICAL MASS."

"BUT WE DIDN'T LOOK ON IT AS A **BLACK** OR **WHITE** WOMEN'S ISSUE; WOMEN NEEDED TERMINATION OF PREGNANCIES AND THERE WAS A *unity* CREATED BY WOMEN WHO WERE DESPERATE."**

* PSEUDONYM
** SEE BIBLIOGRAPHY

I just can't afford another child.

My family will throw me out if I have a child out of wedlock.

I'm about to go to college. I can't have a child!

I just don't want children.

THERE WERE MANY REASONS FOR WOMEN TO SEEK ABORTIONS. JANE **NEVER** ASKED WHAT THE REASONS WERE — THEY JUST MADE SURE A WOMAN WAS CERTAIN SHE WANTED THE ABORTION AND WASN'T BEING FORCED INTO IT BY HER FAMILY OR PARTNER.

MANY JANES WERE MOTHERS THEMSELVES AND DID NOT SEE **MOTHERHOOD** AND **ABORTION** AS *diametrically opposed*.

I can't work this weekend.

We're taking the kids to see their grandma.

BEING A MOTHER WAS VERY IMPORTANT TO ME. MUCH OF WHAT MADE IT SUCH A PLEASURE AND SO COMFORTABLE WAS THE **CHOICE.** I'VE HAD AN ABORTION; I'VE ALSO HAD AN ADOPTIVE DAUGHTER. SO IN SOME WAYS I REPRESENT **THE WHOLE SPECTRUM.**

IT'S A CONTRADICTORY WORLD AND THERE AREN'T SIMPLE ANSWERS, BUT THERE HAS TO BE AN ABILITY TO MAKE **CHOICES.** —JEANNE GALATZER-LEVY

IT'S TEMPTING TO VIEW JANE AS A *legend* OF THE WOMEN'S LIBERATION MOVEMENT, BUT FORMER JANES REFUSE THE IDEA THAT THE GROUP WAS SOME **SPECIAL PRODUCT** OF **HISTORY.**

ALTHOUGH WE WERE FOSTERED AND BOLSTERED BY THE **POLITICS** OF OUR MOVEMENT, WOMEN HAVE *always* BEEN DOING THIS, SO THE NOTION THAT A GRAND POLITICAL HAPPENING IN THE WORLD IS REQUIRED FOR WOMEN TO TAKE ACTION, I THINK IS A LITTLE WRONG-HEADED...

IT MAKES JANE AND ITS MEMBERS TOO DIFFERENT FROM OTHER WOMEN, AND IT'S BEEN MY EXPERIENCE — NOT ONLY THEN BUT EVER SINCE — THAT THERE'S A LOT OF **GOOD STUFF** GOING ON. — JUDITH ARCANA

AS JANE CONTINUED THEIR WORK IN CHICAGO, THE **PRO-CHOICE** MOVEMENT WAS GROWING AROUND THE COUNTRY.

SEVERAL STATES MADE **ABORTION LEGAL.**

THEN THE LANDMARK **ROE v. WADE** IN 1973 MADE ABORTION LEGAL *nationwide* IN THE FIRST THREE MONTHS OF PREGNANCY.

What do we do now?

Let's keep going. Doctors don't have half the respect or experience we do.

And what about late-term pregnancies?

We can't. We'll be liable for practicing without a license.

So? What we've been doing has been illegal this whole time — what's the difference?

JANE MEMBERS HAD BECOME **EXPERIENCED** IN PROVIDING ABORTIONS WHERE MANY MEDICAL PRACTICES WERE **NOT.** WOMEN REPORTED FEELING UNCOMFORTABLE AND DISRESPECTED AT PHYSICIANS' CLINICS, WHERE THEY HAD BEEN RELAXED AND IN CONTROL WITH JANE. BUT IN THE END, THE **ILLEGALITY** OF PRACTICING WITHOUT A LICENSE WAS TOO RISKY.

AFTER ROE, THE GROUP FOLDED.

Roe v. Wade was not exactly a **bargain** to begin with. A lot of people don't realize that Roe was not actually about women being able to determine what they needed or wanted to do; it was about doctors being able to make the **decisions.**

SINCE THE RULING, **ATTITUDES** TOWARD ABORTION HAVE CHANGED.

JANE WANTED TO *demystify* THE PROCEDURE.

BUT IN MANY PARTS OF SOCIETY, ABORTION IS STILL CONSIDERED **TABOO** AND WOMEN ARE LEFT **UNSUPPORTED.**

THIS *wasn't* THE FUTURE OF REPRODUCTIVE CARE THAT THE JANES HAD WORKED SO HARD TO CREATE.

NOW, OPPOSITION FROM A FORCEFUL **ANTI-ABORTION** MOVEMENT HAS CHANGED THE WAY ABORTION IS SPOKEN ABOUT, INFLUENCING WOMEN'S **FEELINGS,** TRESPASSING ON THEIR RIGHT TO **PRIVACY.** AND EXERTING PRESSURE ON POLITICIANS TO **INFRINGE** ON WOMEN'S HEALTHCARE IN ORDER TO WIN VOTES.

In many states, it is as difficult to get an abortion **NOW** as it was **BEFORE** Roe v. Wade.

Women now have *feelings* about the fetus that I do **NOT** share.

The anti-abortion movement has managed in the past four decades, quite brilliantly, to change the culture, the mindset, the thinking, and even the feelings:

the *emotional* response to **abortion, motherhood, pregnancy.**

Their radically violent wing is very active and EXTREMELY DANGEROUS, so the danger to women who are attempting to do the ~~good work~~ now comes not only from the officials— the cops and the politicians— but also from the **serious bad guys.**

STOP
PROTECT LIFE
CHILD
MURDERERS
Pro Life
CHOOSE LIFE
BABIES ARE MURDERED INSIDE
LET YOUR BABY LIVE

DEVELOPING
PROTESTS AT HEALTH CLINIC
NEWS

THE DENVER POST

3
INSIDE THE COLORADO SPRINGS PLANNED PARENTHOOD ATTACK

3 DEAD, 9 WOUNDED

I'M REALLY VERY *encouraged*, DESPITE EVERYTHING. THERE'S AN ENORMOUS AMOUNT OF **ANGER** AND **PUSHBACK** — THERE'S A LOT OF UPPITY WOMEN OUT THERE! I'M SEEING THEM MOVING US FORWARD. I'M FINDING IT A VERY *exciting* TIME FOR WOMEN.

THE THING ABOUT THE WOMEN IN JANE IS WE WERE PERFECTLY ORDINARY PEOPLE; IT'S A MATTER OF, YOU *PUSH* ORDINARY PEOPLE FAR ENOUGH AND ORDINARY PEOPLE DO **EXTRAORDINARY THINGS**.

—JEANNE GALATZER-LEVY

JUDITH ARCANA —

I'M ACTUALLY *hopeful*, IF YOU CAN BELIEVE IT, BECAUSE THE YOUNG ONES ARE **SO SMART**. THEY'RE TOUGH AND THEY **REALLY REALLY** ARE PISSED OFF. THERE AREN'T MILLIONS OF THEM YET, BUT THERE ARE **THOUSANDS** AND **THOUSANDS** ALL OVER THE COUNTRY, AND *THEY'RE DOING IT!* AND I JUST THINK:

Let's → **OKAY!** ← *get going here!*

UNDUE BURDENS

How U.S. reproductive rights law fails poor people

by Hallie Jay Pope

When we talk about abortion and the law in the U.S., most people probably think of <u>Roe v. Wade</u>.

In that landmark case, the Supreme Court decided that the 14th Amendment protects the right to have an abortion.

> What someone does with their uterus is a private choice between them and their doctor!

> Woohoo!

We the People

U.S. Constitution

A uterus

But the Court said that right had **limits**...

> "The right of personal privacy includes the abortion decision, but this right is **not** unqualified and must be considered against important state interests in regulation."

Justice Harry Blackmun

The <u>Roe</u> Court set up a test for evaluating abortion restrictions based on the trimesters of a pregnancy, weighing the pregnant person's* interests against the interests of the state.

First trimester:
The state can't interfere with the pregnant person's decision to have an abortion.

Second trimester on:
The state can impose regulations that reasonably relate to the pregnant person's health.

Viability:
The state can ban abortions not needed for health reasons in order to protect "potential life."

*Why am I saying "person" instead of "woman"? Transgender men and gender-non-conforming people can get pregnant too! And they often face additional hurdles to accessing reproductive care.

Years later in <u>Planned Parenthood v. Casey</u>, the Court replaced <u>Roe</u>'s trimester framework with the test used until 2022: a law restricting abortion was unconstitutional if it imposed an "undue burden" on the person seeking to terminate their pregnancy.

<u>Roe</u> and its progeny were often crucial tools for protecting reproductive rights in the courts.

In 2016 in <u>Whole Woman's Health v. Hellerstedt</u>, the Supreme Court struck down two Texas TRAP* laws under the undue burden test.

"It is beyond rational belief that [these laws] could genuinely protect the health of women..."

Justice Ginsburg, concurring

Then President Trump appointed three anti-choice Justices during his term, and the Court overturned <u>Roe</u> in 2022.

Sad

But even when they were still good law, the <u>Roe</u> line of cases fell short of creating a truly meaningful right to choose, in part because of a different set of laws: **funding restrictions**.

TOLL

*TRAP = targeted regulation of abortion providers

Since the 1970s, Congress has been attaching a rider to federal appropriations bills that **bans the use of federal funds for abortions** (except when the pregnancy is life-threatening or the result of rape or incest).*

1976
This is a great idea!

1994
Sticking with this plan.

2014
Yup still cool with this.

Thanks to this provision, known as the **Hyde Amendment**, it is extremely difficult for Medicaid recipients to obtain safe, legal abortions, even when such procedures are constitutionally protected.

With private insurance:

That'll be $525.**

Here's my insurance card.

With Medicaid:

That'll be $525.

Wellllllp that's more than a quarter of my monthly income.

In other words, the right to have an abortion is not meaningfully available to you if you're poor.

Furthermore, the Hyde Amendment disproportionately affects people of color.

"The Hyde Amendment is designed to **deprive poor and minority women** of the constitutional right to choose abortion."

Justice Thurgood Marshall, dissenting in Harris v. McRae (1980).

The Supreme Court has already ruled that the Hyde Amendment is constitutional, and despite President Biden's reversal of his support for this measure, Congress included it in the 2022 federal budget.

*Some versions haven't even included the rape or incest exceptions, but the most recent ones have.
**In 2018, a first-trimester abortion cost anywhere from $75 to $3000.

While the Hyde Amendment made <u>Roe</u> an empty promise for poor people in the U.S., the Mexico City Policy demeaned it abroad.

We're the GREATEST!

Everyone should be just like us!

No abortions though.

You might think the U.S. government would have wanted to encourage the international provision of a right it supposedly guaranteed to its own citizens. But the Mexico City Policy did exactly the opposite.

This policy, also known as the Global Gag Rule, has been enforced by every Republican president since Reagan.

Trump's version was the broadest yet.

Under Trump's version of the rule, the U.S. would not give **any** international health funds** to NGOs that "perform or actively promote abortion as a method of family planning in other nations."

Given your condition, you may want to consider having an aborti---

NO MORE FUNDING FOR YOU!

*Like his Democratic predecessors, Biden rescinded the Mexico City Policy when he took office.
**Past versions applied only to international family planning funds.

Obviously Trump's version of the Mexico City Policy impacted abortion providers abroad, decreasing funding for reproductive healthcare and making it even more difficult for poor people to obtain safe abortions.

But it **also** affected NGOs that never perform abortions, organizations that focus on fighting threats like HIV/AIDS or cancer and that merely provide information about abortion as a family planning method.

Ironically, some countries' abortion rates **increase** whenever the Mexico City Policy is in effect...probably because groups that provide contraceptives lose the funding to do so.

Even though <u>Roe</u> is no longer good law, these successful efforts to undermine the constitutional right to choose continue to serve as an important reminder.

The courts can be a useful tool for promoting reproductive justice. But without political will behind them, legal decisions may become empty promises for the people who need them the most.

Together, **we have the power** to protect our rights and each other, no matter what the law says.

Okay, this is **Anna Sellheim** and this is **MY MOTHER'S STORY.**

Now?

Yeah, go!

So I guess this all started with your father in the 70s. We had just moved in together.

Dad & I always used contraceptives. I had used an IUD that tore my body apart and the pill was too much.

So I used a diaphragm.

And one morning I woke up and knew I was pregnant.

For every pregnancy I have been aware, almost immediately, that I had a baby inside me.

I had never thought about having children and Dad didn't want any because he had lost contact with his daughter from a previous marriage and it had been very painful.

It was a life, I could feel it. But I didn't think through the ramifications.

Dad said: You have to have an abortion. We haven't been together that long. We don't know where we're going and we haven't settled down.

So, with little thought I had one, but it was emotionally devastating.

WAITING ROOM POLICY

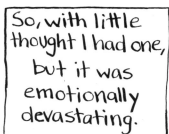

We continued our relationship and committed to each other without even saying it.

I got pregnant again and had a miscarriage.

You have to understand, no one talked to me about anything. I didn't even know what a miscarriage was, I had to look it up. And not on the internet.

And I told Dad: If I get pregnant again I'm having the baby.

And he didn't say anything.

HAHAHA Okay! I don't know what he thought.

God knows, I thought every time I looked at him I got pregnant. Even though I used the diaphragm.

So I got pregnant again.

It was wonderful. It was everything I thought it would be, I loved it.

So we had your brother and Dad loved it. He was ecstatic.

We were living in Maine but Dad wanted to leave so he moved to DC to start a company with a friend.

I moved to NYC and only saw him on weekends.

Why did you move to NYC instead of DC? I got a job there. I wouldn't go anywhere without a job. I was an executive in NYC.

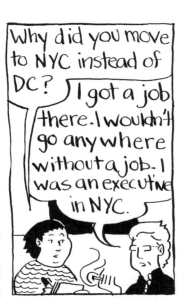

I got pregnant again. It didn't make sense to have the baby because I was, essentially, living as a single mother.

My sister went with me to get an abortion. And it was emotionally very difficult because Dad wasn't there.

Soon after that I moved to DC to be with Dad, and I told him:

I am having the next child. You know I'll get pregnant again

So I'm telling you now, if you don't do something I'm having another baby!

And we did!

HAHAHA!

And you were impossible. You were definitely **IT**.

But you were adorable and wonderful too.

So dad had a vasectomy. He didn't want 3 children. He originally didn't want any!

And I've told you this story:

Hey Terry! How ya doin?

I'll tell you how I'm doing—

I just got clipped!

Yeah, I've told many of my friends that story because it's hilarious!

That was your father!

So why are you Pro-choice?

I'm a feminist.

I know but...I guess I'm just surprised by the language you're using.

You're referring to all of these pregnancies as children. Even the terminated ones.

Pro-choice people are careful to call them fetuses or—

But I get to choose!

I made my choices with and without my husband. It's my body, I get to do whatever I want with it!

Lawmakers get the hell out of my life!

And that's why I took you and your brother to pro-choice rallies, so I could show that you could have children and still be pro-choice.

Women get to choose. It's nobody else's business.

I was 22.

My Voice, My Choice

Story by
Brittany Mostiller
Illustration by
Lilly Taing

I already had three daughters, and I just couldn't afford another child at the time.

—physically,

emotionally, financially.

I wanted so much more for my kids.

The decision to have an abortion was the easy part

It was going to cost $900.

—but I just couldn't afford it.

I was working part-time at a grocery store,

and that was more than I made in a month.

I was just beginning to understand just how hard it is to navigate this world

as a young Black woman and mother.

Paying for my abortion, requesting time off from work,

disclosing my decision to others whom I had to borrow money,

and dealing with the shame was the hard part.

I had gotten a list of resources of different abortion clinics and funds and started calling.

The Chicago Abortion Fund (CAF) gave me $300 for my procedure, which brought me to be just $100 short of what I'd already come up.

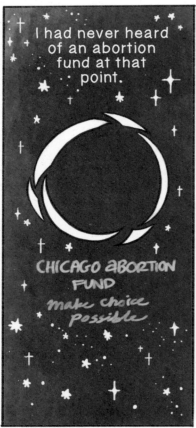

I had never heard of an abortion fund at that point.

CHICAGO ABORTION FUND

make choice possible

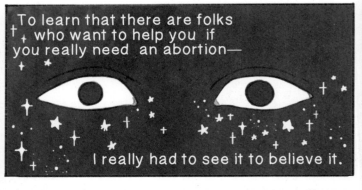

To learn that there are folks who want to help you if you really need an abortion—

I really had to see it to believe it.

But I remember feeling relief and trusting that I could see

that it was going to be OK.

Shortly after the procedure, I got a call from CAF

asking if I wanted to learn more about them.

What kept me going back to meetings was learning about reproductive justice.

I learned that a lot of things I was thinking about on my own,

as a young Black mother on the South Side of Chicago,

and the oppressions I faced, struggled and battled with as a woman and person of color.

Abortion care, poverty, education—all these social justice issues are intertwined.

I saw all these systems of oppression,

and knew I couldn't walk away from this.

You have to be secure in knowing what you need to be healthy and well.

Reproductive justice is the decision to parent

or not parent in a way that feels safe for you.

It will always be tied to feeling safe in your surroundings.

We have to do our part, big or small, but we have to do something and we have to fight for justice.

These aren't difficult conversations, they are necessary conversations.

there's so much stigma, and it just makes people feel shameful, but no.

It makes sense that people don't know about these resources,

I was a mother of three

and now I'm a mother of four.

I love my daughters to the moon and back.

the first time, at the age of 17, and the last time, at the age of 28.

I'm so unapologetic about my decision to have an abortion, my decision to become a parent,

I'm unapologetic about being black. I'm unapologetic about reproductive justice.

Immediately after the procedure, I felt relief and joy because I had already made this plan

to finish school and to try to move forward in my life and do what's best for me and my children.

and I felt like with an unintended pregnancy, I couldn't see those plans through with that happening.

So I felt relieved and thankful and grateful for CAF and my mom and sister for supporting me.

I want people who are choosing to come to us at the CAF to know that

I see them.

We see them.

First and foremost,

We support them.

they are not alone.

I affirm them.

Just know that it's OK. It's actually OK.

The Unruly mob

Written by Lindsay Rodriguez
Illustrated by Lucy Haslam

I joined the board of my local abortion fund in 2012, after Texas stripped Planned Parenthood of funding

I felt incredibly frustrated and alone watching the people in my majority Latinx community

have their

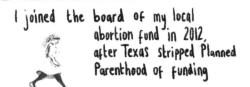

ABORTION ACCESS

continually attacked

and knowing it was the people with the least amount of money and power who got stuck with the worst deal.

I almost

APPLICATION

APPLICATION

never applied.

But I was learning more about the important work funds do to make access available, regardless of where you live or how much you earn.

COURAGE

APPLICATION

And ended up becoming the first Lilith Fund board member in

SAN ANTONIO

That was also the summer my home state of Texas called an "emergency session" to pass a huge law that implemented several unjust restrictions on abortion that would hurt the people who called our hotline the most.

I drove back and forth to Austin, strategizing about what we would do when our already overburdened clinics almost all were shuttered.

That was also the summer I joined thousands of other Texans in unprecedented action to make our disapproval over the law known.

By that time, I was really familiar with talking to people about abortion. I'd spoken to groups about why we need to repeal the Hyde Amendment and have taxpayer funding of abortion. But I'd never in my life experienced the feelings I did the night of Wendy Davis' infamous filibuster

Of course the Republicans called another session and jammed the law through anyway. It was fucked up and ended up at the Supreme Court, where it famously was overturned.

I often say those who are involved in abortion funds end up being part of this movement forever.

Once you've opened the door to understanding the intricate way abortion...

is a flashpoint to so many of the biggest injustices in our world

to racism, poverty, gender injustices, immigration and disability issues, community resources

— it's pretty impossible to close that door again.

The cruelty and repression in Texas has spread, and to be honest: I'm scared.

But one thing I don't worry about anymore is being alone.

COMING OUT

A TEXAS ABORTION STORY
BY SAM ROMERO
AND ERIN LUX

TEXAS IS A HUGE STATE

WE HAVE EVERYTHING FROM DESERT TO WETLANDS

TEXAS IS PART OF THE SOUTH, BUT EL PASO IS PART OF THE SOUTHWEST

SOCIALLY, CULTURALLY, POLITICALLY, EL PASO IS STARKLY DIFFERENT THAN THE REST OF THE STATE

AS A MINORITY, MAJORITY COUNTY, EL PASO IS A SPECIAL PLACE IN THE DESERT CONNECTING TEXAS, MEXICO AND NEW MEXICO

NEW MEXICO

•EL PASO

TEXAS

MEXICO

IT'S MY SAFE HAVEN AND SANCTUARY, CONSISTENTLY RANKED ONE OF THE SAFEST CITIES IN THE U.S.

I HAD NEVER BEEN MUCH INTERESTED OR INFORMED ABOUT POLITICS UNTIL I HAPPENED TO RUN INTO ORGANIZERS WHO EXCITEDLY EXPLAINED HOW THEY WANTED TO TURN TEXAS BLUE

I QUICKLY LEARNED ABOUT WENDY DAVIS + HER AMAZING FILIBUSTER

SHE ATTEMPTED TO STOP A AN ANTI-CHOICE BILL THAT WOULD SHUT DOWN MANY ABORTION CLINICS UNDER THE GUISE OF "SAFETY"

IN A STATE LIKE TEXAS, THIS MAKES A HUGE IMPACT BECAUSE IT LEFT SOME WITH THE ONLY OPTION OF TRAVELING HOURS TO THE NEAREST CLINIC

I WAS LUCKY ENOUGH TO HAVE THE OPPORTUNITY TO WORK ON THE WENDY DAVIS CAMPAIGN, HOWEVER, I WAS NOT READY FOR LIVING IN A STATE THAT DIDN'T FEEL LIKE HOME

ON TOP OF EVERYTHING, I FELT SAD

I USED TO CRY EVERY DAY OF THE CAMPAIGN

AS AN OUTSIDER, I FELT I COULD SEE THINGS MORE CLEARLY AND DIFFERENTLY

NOT BECAUSE PEOPLE WERE MEAN TO ME, BUT BECAUSE I FELT TEXAS DESERVED A CHANGE

I WAS IN A COMMUNITY WHERE SOME FELT UNSAFE TO VOICE THEIR POLITICAL OPINIONS

MYSELF INCLUDED

I WAS LITERALLY RAN OFF PEOPLE'S YARDS ON SOME OCCASIONS

IN ONE INSTANCE, AN OLDER WHITE WOMAN CONDESCENDINGLY ASKED IF I KNEW WHERE I WAS AFTER I MENTIONED WENDY DAVIS

SHE SAID IT IN A TONE THAT IMPLIED I SHOULD LEAVE

AS A YOUNG LATINA, IT FELT HARSH, UNCALLED FOR, AND CRUEL

IT'S A WEIRD THING TO FEEL LIKE EVEN YOUR
SPIRITUALITY IS BEING POLICED

IT BROUGHT TO ATTENTION MANY THINGS I TOOK FOR GRANTED IN EL PASO, SUCH AS MY FREEDOM OF SPEECH, RELIGION + OVERALL SAFETY

WHEN IT CAME TO ABORTION, IT WAS ALWAYS A GENDERED CONVERSATION

IN TEXAS, EVEN THE DEMOCRATS ARE MODERATE

I MET A LOT OF SINGLE ISSUE VOTERS (THE SINGLE ISSUE BEING ABORTION)

PEOPLE WHO REFUSED TO HAVE A RATIONAL CONVERSATION

PRAY TO END ABORTION

STOP ABORTION

BODIES ARE ...ERED

Defund

FOR SOME, IT'S ABOUT WOMEN WHO NEED TO KEEP THEIR LEGS SHUT

OR THE WOMAN'S JOB TO PRACTICE SAFE SEX

IT WAS AS IF MEN WERE COMPLETELY ABSOLVED FROM THE PROCESS

SOME PEOPLE THOUGHT IT WOULD BE HELPFUL TO DECIDE IF THERE WAS A WAY TO FILTER AND JUDGE WHO SHOULD HAVE AN ABORTION ON A CASE-BY-CASE BASIS

AS IF ONLY SOME PEOPLE "DESERVED" ABORTIONS

FOR ME, DURING THE ENTIRE CAMPAIGN I TRIED NOT TO DEBATE PEOPLE

IT WAS A LOSING BATTLE, PLUS I'M NOT ONE TO ARGUE OR BE CONFRONTATIONAL

HOWEVER, THE SHEER HATRED PEOPLE HAD FOR WENDY DAVIS WAS POWERFUL

LIKE THERE WAS THIS INNATE SENSE OF OFFENSE PEOPLE TOOK FROM ONLY HEARING HER NAME

I FELT LIKE PEOPLE WERE MEAN TO ME BECAUSE THEY DIDN'T LIKE HER

IT WAS STRANGE TO BE THE TOOL PEOPLE USED TO TAKE OUT THEIR ANGER ON

IT ALSO CAME BACK TO RELIGION, AS IF COMPASSION AND SYMPATHY DON'T APPLY TO THOSE THEY DEEM UNWORTHY

(THIS IS DEFINITELY RELATED TO THE PATRIARCHY)

MY ABORTIONS

COMIC BY
LAURA LANNES

DRAWING
CANDICE RUSSELL'S
REAL STORY

I GOT PREGNANT AT 21.

I HAD TROUBLE KEEPING MY NEOPET ALIVE, SO THE CHOICE WAS CLEAR.

I GOT AN ABORTION AT 21.

I DON'T SEE WHY I SHOULD BE EMBARRASSED ABOUT THIS. I WAS TOO YOUNG, BROKE AND UNINSURED.

I'D EAT TACO BELL FOR WEEKS STRAIGHT BECAUSE I DIDN'T WANT TO GO TO THE STORE AND BUY DISH SOAP.

IN 2013, I WAITED IN LINE FOR 12 HOURS TO TESTIFY IN FRONT OF A STATE SENATE PANEL AGAINST THE PASSING OF HB2.

I TOLD THEM ABOUT HOW MY MOTHER DECIDED AT THE LAST MOMENT NOT TO TERMINATE HER PREGNANCY WITH ME.

AND I TOLD THEM MY OWN ABORTION STORY.

BUT IN THE END, AS WE ALL KNOW, HB2 PASSED.

OVER THE NEXT YEAR, LIKE MANY TEXANS, I SPENT A LOT OF TIME FIGHTING AGAINST THE BILL AND ITS RESTRICTIONS—

NO TO HB2

RESTRICTIONS WHICH I NEVER THOUGHT WOULD AFFECT ME. BUT THEN...

I GOT PREGNANT AT 30.

WHEN I REALIZED IT, I WAS FAR ALONG ENOUGH TO NEED A SURGICAL ABORTION.

CLINICS IN THE DFW AREA HAD NO APPOINTMENTS. SO WE DECIDED I'D HAVE THE PROCEDURE IN CALIFORNIA, WHERE MY THEN-PARTNER LIVED.

I TOOK A SUPER HIGH INTEREST PAYDAY LOAN IN ORDER TO AFFORD THE TRIP. IT PUT ME DEEP IN DEBT.

STILL, I'M A LUCKY WOMAN. MOST PEOPLE IN THE RIO GRANDE VALLEY CAN'T JUST JUMP ON A PLANE TO GET AN ABORTION.

SO I WENT TO CALIFORNIA. I GOT AN ABORTION. I CAME HOME.

LIFE CARRIED ON. LIKE IT DOES.

SUDDENLY IT WAS THE ANNI-VERSARY OF THE PASSING OF HB2. I STARTED RECEIVING

EMAILS ASKING FOR PERSONAL ACCOUNTS OF THE PASSING OF HB2

EACH EMAIL STABBED AT MY HEART A LITTLE. AND EACH EMAIL WAS PROMPTLY DELE-TED.

IT WAS HARD FOR ME TO ADMIT THAT I HAD NEVER SEEN MY CHOICE AS VALID.

ONE DAY, A WORK COLLEAGUE CONFIDED IN ME THAT SHE WAS

PREGNANT.

AND I'M NOT SURE WHAT TO DO.

HAVE YOU ACTUALLY HAD AN ABORTION?

UH...

MY FIRST INSTINCT WAS TO TELL HER THE STORY I HAD PRACTICED SO MANY TIMES.

I WAS YOUNG.

THE ONE I TOLD TO THE SENATE COMMITTEE.

I WAS BROKE.

THE ONE THAT WAS MUCH EASIER FOR PEOPLE TO SWALLOW BECAUSE IT PROVIDED JUSTIFICATIONS FOR MY ACTIONS.

I WAS JUST NOT READY.

BUT SHE WAS 33, A PROFESSIONAL WITH A CAREER AND A LIFE IN ORDER. NONE OF THAT APPLIED TO HER.

SO I TOLD HER BOTH STORIES. ABOUT HOW I WAS 21, POOR, JUST NOT READY...

AND ABOUT HOW I WAS 30, AND I DIDN'T WANT TO BE A MOTHER.

I DON'T WANT TO BE A MOTHER EITHER. I NEVER HAVE. I DIDN'T THINK IT WAS NORMAL.

I BELIEVE ONE OF THE SINGLE MOST POWERFUL THINGS WE CAN DO TO END THE STIGMA AROUND ABORTION IS TO TELL OUR STORIES.

WE DON'T OWE ANYONE EXPLANATIONS.

AS LONG AS WE KEEP TELLING OUR STORIES.

WE WILL BE HEARD.

The Outcasts
Written by Heidi Williamson
Art by Cielo Krase

Atlanta, 2037, Cell Block C, Fulton County Jail.
The world has become a hostile place for women, as their sexual activities and reproductive health decisions are monitored daily. Women are jailed for crimes against the state if they do not comply with very strict guidelines about procreation and pregnancy. Such crimes are punishable by death.

You ready?

Ella Shivers, Age 32, Convicted of Crimes against the State, Rule 4.12: Illegal abortion.

Sí.

Christina Ellis, Age 24, Convicted of Crimes against the State, Rule 4.22: Suspected miscarriage.

Marta Jimenez, Age 41, Convicted of Crimes against the State, Rule 4.15: Failure to comply with compulsory monitoring of pregnancy.

Right Here.

Good morning, ladies. It is time for your appointment with the death chamber. Step out and cross your wrists.

Dining Hall, Underground Headquarters, just outide of Atlanta, GA

Good news, the prison has called off the search. You are free! Mother Jones will be down to greet you shortly.

TAP TAP TAP TAP TAP TAP TAP

As we speak, homes are being raided, and the president has closed the border to prevent families from leaving.

Our nation is in a state of disarray. Your work will help everyone heal. It will help our community control its own destiny.

Homes are being *raided*?! But why?

Because of power and control. Women are being jailed and interrogated about their sexual practices, their pregnancies and other crimes against the state. Much like you were.

Don't look defeated.

Your profession has been outlawed, but it is an opportunity. A law that is morally unjust must be defied. *And we will do just that.*

Yes, we will.

THE SANCTITY OF Life

WORDS: CATHY CAMPER
ART: JENNIFER CAMPER

FIRST, TEXAS ORDERS BURIALS OF ABORTED FETUSES.

LITTLE CLARA
OCT. 3-27 2017
OUR ANGEL

SIX MONTHS LATER OKLAHOMA RULES UNFERTILIZED EGGS, MENSTRUAL PRODUCTS, AND BLOOD MUST RECEIVE DEATH CERTIFICATES AND BURIALS.

TAMPON COFFINS

ON SALE

CHEAP!

THE NEXT YEAR LOUISIANA DECLARES ALL SPENT HUMAN SPERM REQUIRES AUTHORIZED BURIALS.

TRUCKLOADS OF SPERM ROAM THE LAND SEARCHING FOR GRAVES.

TWO YEARS LATER WISCONSIN RULES THAT ANY PAST THOUGHTS OF PROCREATION REQUIRE CREMATION.

INTO THE FUNERAL PYRE!

LOVE SONGS

LOVE LETTER

EVENTUALLY THE SEPARATED STATES OF AMERICA DECLARE ALL UNSPROUTED SEEDS MUST RECEIVE BURIALS.

SIGH...

MAYBE I COULD BURY MY TAMPONS IN THE SEEDS?

BODY & SOUL, SCIENCE & RELIGION:
ALL CROWDED INTO ONE UTERUS
PHYSICAL AND SPIRITUAL MILESTONES OF EMBRYOLOGICAL AND FETAL DEVELOPMENT.

BY KRIOTA WILLBERG

1ST TRIMESTER (WEEKS 0-12)

Conception/Fertilization occurs when a **sperm** fuses with an **egg.**

Woo hoo!

Rats!

A fertilized egg is called a **zygote.**

(Egg, sperm, zygote, and souls not drawn to scale.)

CONCEPTION/FERTILIZATION

Conception and **fertilization** are often used **synonymously.** We'll use them that way too.

Ensoulment is when the human-to-be gets a soul.

Hey you! Leggo my eggo!

Hindus, Sikhs, Christians, and Buddhists say the zygote is imbued with a soul **at the moment of conception.** But there is not unanimous agreement on this between all religions.

EMBRYONIC PERIOD

starts 3 WEEKS post conception

The embryo forms 3 types of tissues: **ectoderm, mesoderm,** and **endoderm.** They begin to fold around each other.

Starts out looking like this,

then this,

then this.

Magnified

Unmagnified*

•   •   •

4 WEEKS post conception

By DAY 22 the embryo has a heart tube (HT) that contracts and pushes blood around.

The tube is made from **mesoderm.** It will fold and loop to develop into a four-chambered heart.

22 Days

HT

Invisible embryo

24 Days

HT

25 Days

Un-magnified*

•

*Sizes are approximate because these embryos are TINY!

The philosopher, ARISTOTLE (384-322 BCE), used **binary** language to describe a person's **sex**. I have no idea how he used language to describe **gender**. He believed that **male ensoulment occured at 40 days.**

Rumors say Aristotle said the soul of a human starts as a **vegetable,**

...progresses to **animal,**

...and then becomes a **person** at 40 or 90 days.

This is a "male" embryo around 42 days old.

Here is a close up of his face.

How do we know he's male? Because he has a **soul!**

Which one is the **lentil** and which one is the **embryo?**

This will be a **nostril!**

An 8 WEEK OLD embryo is around **2 inches long.**

The external genitalia start developing although they are **not apparent yet.**

An embryo beginning to grow a penis **has a soul** at this time. (Per Aristotle)

An embryo beginning to grow a clitoris and labia majora **does NOT** have a soul at this time. (Per Aristotle)

The FETAL PERIOD starts at 9 WEEKS post conception.

Today I am a fetus!

2 1/2 inches

12 WEEKS post conception

This fetus has been **peeing** into its amniotic fluid for 1 week.

Me too!

2ND TRIMESTER WEEKS 13-28

A fetus with a **clitoris** gets a soul at 90* days, or 12 weeks and 6 days!

Hmph!

*According to St. Augustine, this happens at 80 days.

ARISTOTLE

13 WEEKS post conception

Hehe! It tickles!*

*This is a joke. It is not educational. At 13 weeks the nervous system (formed by the **ectoderm**) is **not** developed enough to feel tickled, that's why this is funny.

120 DAYS or 17 WEEKS PLUS 1 DAY post conception

From an **Islamic perspective**, "the spirit is breathed in after 120 days."

The lungs, formed from **endoderm**, are in the early stages of developing specific tubes and tissues for gas exchange. They **cannot function outside the womb** at this time.

Future air saccules

In the **last trimester** the lungs develop air **saccules**. After birth they will mature into air sacs called **alveoli**. In order for lungs to work, the saccules and alveoli need to have an internal coating of **surfactant**. It **keeps the saccules** and alvioli **from collapsing** and sticking together after exhalation.

Air saccules (future alveoli)

The time at which a mother starts to feel her fetus move in her uterus is called

QUICKENING.

Note: In order to accommodate dramatic "action lines," the uteri on this page are missing structures vital to pregnancy (such as the placenta.)

Throughout history quickening has been sited as the **indication of ensoulment**.

Some people claimed to know the **gender** of the fetus based on aspects of quickening.

In the **United States** during the **19th century** abortion during the first trimester was generally **morally acceptable**.

Woman's body.

There was not consensus on the **precise moment** of ensoulment, but it was generally agreed that **prior** to ensoulment the embryo was considered a part of the **mother's** body.

After ensoulment the embryo became a **person**.

Woman's body.

Someone else's body.

At 20 WEEKS the fetus is around 7 1/2" long.

Quickening starts anywhere from 16–20 WEEKS post conception.

I'm an obstetrician. Ensoulment is not my area of expertise.

Contemporary medical sources write about ensoulment in the context of **bioethical** discussions about **pregnancy** and/or **abortion** from various religious perspectives.

VIABILITY

A fetus is VIABLE when it can **survive outside the womb.**

> I'm not viable unless I weigh **at least** as much as two cups of raw hamburger!

> That's **500 grams**; just over 1 pound!

With **intensive** medical technology, drugs, and care, some babies **might** survive out of the womb as early as 21 WEEKS post conception.

> I can't **breathe** on my own.

> That means I am viable **only** if I have **access** to expensive machines.

It can't be done now, but in the **future**, if a fetus is **conceived** and **gestated** in a laboratory, does that mean it's **viable from conception?**

Complications of **preterm birth** can include: respiratory distress; infections; poor neurological conditions such as cerebral palsy; and more. Some of these are **permanent.**

Healthy babies born 26 WEEKS after conception have a **90% chance** of surviving **without** impairment. Babies born at this time weigh almost 2 1/4 pounds, which equals 1,000 grams.

"Viability" becomes a **fluid term** as medical technology advances.

"Born and Forgotten"

story
Dr. Katherine Brown
& Andrew Carl

art
Seth Smith

Ms. Hendricks, the doctor is ready for you.

Hello, Ms. Hendricks. What brings you here today?

Um...I need an abortion?

Well, when did you first find out you were pregnant?

I, um, took a test five days ago.

Okay, how many pregnancies have you had in the past?

Two...I have two kids.

Now is this something you're sure of, or—

I'm sure.

We can provide medical and surgical abortions here.

But before we start, there are some things I'm required by law to discuss with you.

These pamphlets have been prepared by the state to provide "medical information" and contact resources for "options" counseling.

What's in there is dictated by anti-abortion legislation.

I'm required to tell you about some of their contents...

...but I also want to point out how misleading they can be.

Medical research has not pinpointed any moment when a fetus starts being able to perceive pain.

We know a fetus' sensory system develops between 23 and 30 weeks' gestation. It's unlikely that those senses are able to be interpreted before 29 weeks at the earliest.

I have to bring this up so that you know what to make of how these pamphlets' talk about an "unborn baby's" pain.

I want to assure you, these warnings come from political actors without concern for medical fact.

I wonder how much those "political actors" care about my kids' pain?

RESOURCE
DIRECTORY
A Woman's Right to Know

I also have to provide this contact info, developed by the state, for resources related to your pregnancy and alternatives to abortion.

The "pregnancy centers" recommended here present themselves as full-service health and counseling centers for abortion, pregnancy, and child care...

...but they're actually anti-choice organizations. So be careful.

The information you'd receive there is unscientific, and designed to coerce your decision.

state law also requires you to know the "range of emotional effects of undergoing an abortion...

oh.

...which can include suicidal thoughts, depression, and anxiety."

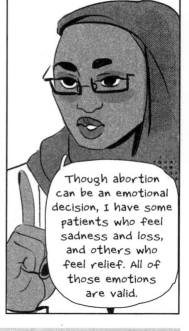

Though abortion can be an emotional decision, I have some patients who feel sadness and loss, and others who feel relief. All of those emotions are valid.

How you feel afterward is most connected to your mental health beforehand.

My family's dealing with a lot already... I just need to be able to take care of the kids I have now.

Just like every medical procedure, abortion has risks, but it's safer than these materials make it seem. In fact, carrying a fetus to term is over 20 times more likely to result in death. These numbers are still both very low. We'll go through all the potential risks before your procedure...

nod nod

...but for now I just want to make sure you aren't misled.

For example, this booklet talks about abortion's link to breast cancer.

But there is absolutely no proven association between abortion and risk of breast cancer. The National Cancer Institute and experts around the world have come to the same conclusion: there's just no connection.

So now someone cares about whether I get cancer, huh...

That will be $200 for your pap smear.

What?!

Sorry, without insurance...

I'm sorry that state law requires me to show you this ultrasound. You can cover your eyes or look away.

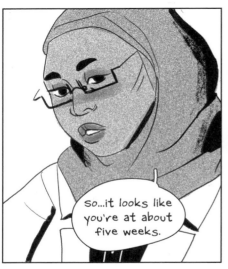

So...it looks like you're at about five weeks.

If it were one week from now, I would have to tell you that we can't perform this procedure.

You'd have to go out of state.

Am I supposed to feel like a bad person right now?

Like I wouldn't care about hurting an innocent baby?

In ongoing news, Flint's water crisis continues to endanger its community. Children with elevated blood lead levels have exhibited developmental delay, weight loss, hearing loss, fatigue, and seizures.

SATURDAY MORNING

I REGRET MY ABORTION

GOD IS PRO LIFE

STOP KILLI BABI

ADOPTION IS AN OPTION

Author: Benita Ulisano
Artist: Laura Martin

sigh

Morning, Lynda.

Looks like we already have company.

Yeah, they got here at like 4AM. Anyway, here's your supplies—

PRO-CHOICE CLINIC ESCORT

FPA FAMILY PLANNING ASSOCIATES

ABORTION IS WRONG

They Can't Get That From Us.

STEPH KRAFT SHELEY

IN THE UNITED STATES, ORGANIZATIONS THAT PROVIDE HEALTHCARE ARE RUN LIKE FOR-PROFIT BUSINESSES, AND MOST TAKE THE CORPORATE FORM. THE PRECISE STRUCTURE OF THESE BUSINESSES DIFFERS FROM ORGANIZATION TO ORGANIZATION, BUT MOST ARE ARRANGED IN A HIERARCHY WHEREIN EACH LEVEL MUST ACCOUNT TO THE NEXT LEVEL UP FOR ITS FINANCIAL BOTTOM LINE.

HEALTHCARE ORGANIZATIONS ARE INCREASINGLY MOVING TOWARD FULL INTEGRATION, WHICH ALLOWS PATIENTS WITH THE ABILITY TO PAY TO SEEK MOST OF THEIR CARE FROM THE SAME ORGANIZATION. THESE INTEGRATED ORGANIZATIONS ARE CALLED HEALTH SYSTEMS. MANY COMMUNITIES HAVE MULTIPLE HEALTH SYSTEMS, AND MANY HEALTH SYSTEMS OPERATE IN MULTIPLE COMMUNITIES.

THIS STRUCTURE BENEFITS PATIENTS BECAUSE INFORMATION ABOUT THE PATIENT'S HEALTH IS SHARED AUTOMATICALLY BETWEEN THEIR CARE PROVIDERS. THIS HELPS PROVIDERS GET A COMPLETE PICTURE OF THE PATIENT'S HEALTH AT ALL STAGES.

ELECTRONIC PATIENT INFORMATION STORAGE

FAMILY CARE — URGENT CARE — IMAGING CENTER — OB/GYN

THIS THEORETICALLY INCREASES THE QUALITY OF THE CARE PROVIDED.

THIS STRUCTURE ALSO HEAVILY BENEFITS THE HEALTH SYSTEM BY KEEPING MONEY GENERATED BY ALL TYPES OF HEALTH SERVICES FLOWING BACK TO THE HEALTH SYSTEM. THIS INCENTIVIZES HEALTH SYSTEMS TO PROVIDE ALL THE CARE THAT PATIENTS REQUIRE.

HEALTH SYSTEM

CARDIOLOGY ASSO — AMBULATORY SURGICAL CENTER — LABORATORY — H EMERGENCY

EXCEPT, FOR SOME REASON, ABORTION.

HEALTH SYSTEM

FAMILY CARE — OB/GYN — H EMERGENCY

I NEED AN ABORTION.
ARE YOU ACTIVELY DYING?
NO.
WE CAN'T HELP YOU.

I NEED AN ABORTION
I DON'T DO THOSE

I NEED AN ABORTION
I CAN'T DO THAT

I NEED AN ABORTION.

OKAY. FILL THIS OUT AND THEN LET'S TALK.

SEARCH THE WEB

CALL AROUND

ASK FRIENDS

ABORTION PROVIDER

THE VAST MAJORITY OF ABORTIONS ARE PERFORMED IN DEDICATED REPRODUCTIVE HEALTH CLINICS RATHER THAN DOCTORS' OFFICES OR HOSPITALS.

THIS SEGREGATION PERSISTS DESPITE THE FACT THAT ABORTION IS EXTREMELY SAFE AND COMMON.

THE SEPARATION OF ABORTION AND ITS CONSEQUENCES BECAME CLEAR TO ME AS I PURSUED EDUCATIONAL AND PROFESSIONAL OPPORTUNITIES.

WHILE EARNING DEGREES IN LAW

AND HEALTH ADMINISTRATION..

COLLEGE OF LAW

COLLEGE OF PUBLIC HEALTH

BOARD ROOM INDEPENDENT FEMINIST WOMEN'S HEALTH CLINIC

...I SPENT FREE TIME ON AN ABORTION PROVIDER'S BOARD

STUDYING LAW CONVINCED ME THAT THE RIGHT TO LEGAL ABORTION MUST BE PRESERVED.

We the Pe

HEALTH LAW and POLICY 4th Ed.

STUDYING HEALTH ADMINISTRATION, I LEARNED THE BUSINESS OF PROVIDING HEALTHCARE. BUT I FREQUENTLY ENCOUNTERED MESSAGES FROM PROFESSORS AND CLASSMATES SUGGESTING THAT ABORTION IS DEVIANT BEHAVIOR, AND SO UNCOMMON THAT WE NEED NOT DISCUSS IT IN DETAIL.

Strategic Planning & Marketing

ANALYTICS

Revenue Cycle Management

Professional Dress for the Workplace

Health Policy

Public Health

I KNEW, HOWEVER, THAT ABORTION IS A COMMON HEALTH NEED.

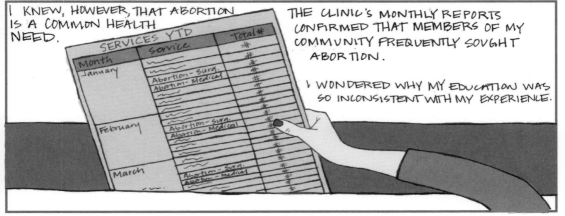

SERVICES YTD

Month	Service	Total #
January	Abortion - Surg.	
	Abortion - Medical	
February	Abortion - Surg.	
	Abortion - Medical	
March	Abortion - Surg.	
	Abortion - Medical	

THE CLINIC'S MONTHLY REPORTS CONFIRMED THAT MEMBERS OF MY COMMUNITY FREQUENTLY SOUGHT ABORTION.

I WONDERED WHY MY EDUCATION WAS SO INCONSISTENT WITH MY EXPERIENCE.

I DID SOME RESEARCH, AND STARTED RAISING THE ISSUE OF ABORTION IN MY CLASSES. THE RESPONSES. THIS PROBING ELICITED FROM THOSE WITH EXPERTISE IN HEALTH CARE HELPED ME UNDERSTAND WHY AND HOW MAINSTREAM HEALTH CARE EXCLUDES ABORTION.

Stigma

ABORTION STIGMA STEMS FROM THE PERCEPTION THAT SOCIETY GENERALLY DISAPPROVES OF ABORTION.

...AND THAT'S WHY HEALTH ADMINS SHOULD BE KNOWLEDGE-ABLE ABOUT ABORTION.

me

THAT'S INTERESTING, BUT IT'S IMPORTANT TO NOTE THAT EVERY ABORTION HURTS SOMEONE, BE IT MOM, DAD OR BABY.

me

PROFESSOR

I DON'T THINK EVERY ABORTION IS A TRAGEDY, BUT WE CAN AGREE TO DISAGREE ON THAT.

COMMUNITY HEALTH CENTER CEO

WE DO A LOT OF BIRTHS FOR THE LOW-INCOME POPULATION

WHAT DO YOU DO WHEN A PATIENT NEEDS AN ABORTION?

me

... YEAH WELL ... IF THAT'S WHAT SHE DECIDES TO DO, SHE CAN'T GET **THAT** FROM US.

I EXPERIENCED ABORTION STIGMA IN THE FORM OF PRESSURE NOT TO USE THE WORD "ABORTION." IT BECAME CLEAR THAT HEARING THE WORD SPOKEN ALOUD MADE STUDENTS AND PROFESSORS UNCOMFORTABLE. ON ONLY ONE OCCASION DID A PROFESSOR INITIATE A DISCUSSION OF ABORTION'S STATUS IN HEALTHCARE, BUT HE ENDED HIS TALK BY VOICING A PERSONAL OBJECTION TO ABORTION. THE RESULT IS THAT FUTURE HEALTH LEADERS LEARNED THAT IF ABORTION MAKES THEM UNCOMFORTABLE, THEY ARE FREE TO IGNORE IT ALTOGETHER.

Religious Directives

SOME HEALTH SYSTEMS ARE OWNED OR SPONSORED BY THE CATHOLIC CHURCH. THESE ORGANIZATIONS OPERATE SUBJECT TO A SET OF DIRECTIVES THAT EXPRESSLY PROHIBIT ABORTION CARE. CATHOLIC HOSPITALS AND HEALTH SYSTEMS ARE THEREFORE PROHIBITED FROM PERFORMING ABORTIONS, SAVE IN SOME CASES WHERE THE PATIENT'S LIFE IS THREATENED.

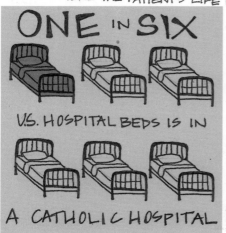

ONE IN SIX

U.S. HOSPITAL BEDS IS IN A CATHOLIC HOSPITAL

NEW HEALTH SYSTEM

MERGER

CATHOLIC HEALTH SYSTEM

SECULAR HEALTH SYSTEM

WHEN HOSPITALS OR HEALTH SYSTEMS MERGE, OR WHEN ONE ACQUIRES ANOTHER, THE RELIGIOUS DIRECTIVES OF ONE HOSPITAL MAY BE APPLIED TO ALL OF THE FACILITIES IN THE NEWLY-FORMED SYSTEM. WHEN THAT HAPPENS, THE NEW PARENT ORGANIZATION MAY FORBID PROVIDERS TO PROVIDE ABORTION CARE.

Unprofitability

BOTH FOR-PROFIT AND NONPROFIT HEALTH SYSTEMS ARE MOTIVATED BY PROFIT. "NO MARGIN NO MISSION" IS A COMMON PHRASE IN DISCUSSIONS ABOUT NONPROFIT HEALTHCARE, AND IT REFERS TO THE IDEA THAT IF AN ORGANIZATION DOESN'T EARN MORE THAN IT SPENDS, IT WILL GO OUT OF BUSINESS, AND THUS UNABLE TO FULFILL ITS CHARITABLE DUTIES.* THEREFORE, HEALTHCARE PROVIDERS STRONGLY PREFER TO OFFER SERVICES THAT CAN GENERATE SUBSTANTIAL REIMBURSEMENTS FROM A PATIENT'S INSURER. PUBLIC AND PRIVATE INSURANCE COVERAGE VARIES AMONG THE STATES, WITH THE MAJORITY PLACING RESTRICTIONS ON ABORTION COVERAGE. THE MAJORITY OF ABORTIONS ARE PAID FOR OUT OF POCKET, AND MANY PATIENTS REQUIRE FINANCIAL ASSISTANCE TO HELP PAY FOR THEIR ABORTIONS.

*"NO MARGIN, NO MISSION" IS TOO OFTEN USED TO JUSTIFY PROFIT-DRIVEN ACTIVITIES THAT ARE INCONSISTENT WITH THE COMMUNITY'S NEEDS.

History

AFTER ROE V. WADE LEGALIZED ABORTION NATIONWIDE, HEALTHCARE PROVIDERS AND COMMUNITY ACTIVISTS HAD TO DECIDE HOW TO ESTABLISH ACCESS TO ABORTION CARE.

MANY MAINSTREAM HOSPITALS AND DOCTORS' OFFICES WERE UNWILLING TO START PROVIDING ABORTIONS...

...SO ADVOCATES AND SUPPORTIVE PHYSICIANS BEGAN SETTING UP SEPARATE CLINICS WHERE THEY COULD PROVIDE ABORTIONS.

THESE TYPICALLY TOOK ONE OF TWO FORMS:

FEMINIST CLINICS

- REJECTION OF PATRIARCHY
- EMPHASIZED WOMAN-CENTERED CARE
- WOMEN TOOK ON PROVIDER ROLES
- PRIORITIZED PATIENT EDUCATION

MEDICAL ABORTION CLINICS

- EMPHASIZED SAFE ABORTION BY TRAINED PHYSICIANS
- ENCOURAGED RESEARCH ON SAFE ABORTION PRACTICES

Schoen, J. (2013)

WHILE MAINSTREAM HEALTHCARE'S REJECTION OF ABORTION CARE WAS THE CAUSE OF ABORTION SEGREGATION, THE RISE OF STANDALONE CLINICS HAS NOT BEEN ENTIRELY NEGATIVE. STANDALONE CLINICS DEVELOPED AS PLACES FOR WOMEN TO ESCAPE THE MALE-DOMINATED AND PATRIARCHAL MEDICAL ESTABLISHMENT. TODAY, MANY STANDALONE CLINICS OPERATE UNDER THE SAME PHILOSOPHY.

THE VALUE OF THESE CLINICS IS SIGNIFICANT, AND WHILE ABORTION SHOULD BE MADE AVAILABLE FROM MAINSTREAM HEALTHCARE PROVIDERS, PATIENTS SHOULD ALWAYS HAVE THE OPTION TO OBTAIN THEIR REPRODUCTIVE HEALTHCARE FROM A STANDALONE CLINIC.

WHAT EFFECT DOES ABORTION SEGREGATION HAVE ON PATIENTS?

CONTRIBUTES TO PATIENT HARASSMENT

ABORTION IS MURDER

MOMMY DON'T KILL ME

I REGRET MY ABORTION

I'LL ADOPT YOUR BABY

GOD WILL JUDGE YOU.

PATIENTS OFTEN HAVE TO PASS HARASSING PROTESTERS IN ORDER TO ENTER ABORTION CLINICS. PROTESTERS WAVE INTIMIDATING SIGNS AND GRUESOME IMAGES. THEY CALL OUT INSULTS, AND SOMETIMES TRY TO PERSUADE PATIENTS TO FOLLOW THEM TO ANOTHER LOCATION WHERE THEY CAN PRESSURE THE PATIENT TO KEEP THEIR PREGNANCY.

PATIENTS SEEKING NO OTHER TYPE OF MEDICAL TREATMENT ARE SUBJECTED TO THIS ABUSE.

IT WOULD BE FAR MORE DIFFICULT FOR PROTESTERS TO SINGLE OUT AND HARASS PATIENTS IF ABORTION CARE WERE INTEGRATED INTO MAINSTREAM HEALTHCARE.

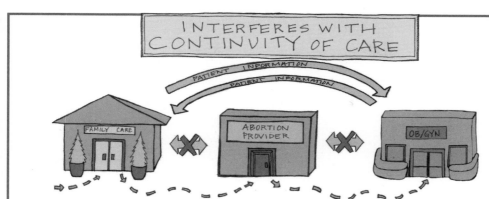

INTERFERES WITH CONTINUITY OF CARE

WHILE RESEARCH SUGGESTS THAT MANY PATIENTS PREFER TO RECEIVE ABORTION CARE FROM THEIR REGULAR HEALTH CARE PROVIDERS, MANY MAINSTREAM PROVIDERS DO NOT OFFER THAT OPTION. PATIENTS WHO ARE FORCED TO SEEK ABORTION FROM OTHER PROVIDERS MAY MISS OUT ON THE BENEFITS ASSOCIATED WITH CONTINUITY OF CARE.

HINDERS ACCESS TO ABORTION

ALTHOUGH ABORTIONS OVERWHELMINGLY (96%) TAKE PLACE IN CLINICS OTHER THAN HOSPITALS AND DOCTORS' OFFICES, 90% OF COUNTIES IN THE UNITED STATES HAVE NO CLINIC THAT PROVIDES ABORTION. IF MAINSTREAM PROVIDERS INCORPORATED ABORTION INTO THEIR PRACTICES, ACCESS WOULD BE GREATLY IMPROVED.

PERPETUATES ABORTION STIGMA

STIGMA IS BOTH A CAUSE AND EFFECT OF ABORTION SEGREGATION. WHEN ABORTION IS TREATED AS IF IT IS NOT A NORMAL PART OF HEALTHCARE, PATIENTS GET THE MESSAGE THAT ABORTION IS NOT A LEGITIMATE OPTION. STIGMA ALSO DETERS PROVIDERS FROM OFFERING ABORTION TO THEIR PATIENTS FOR FEAR OF HARM TO THEIR PROFESSIONAL REPUTATIONS. SIMILARLY, HEALTH SYSTEMS ARE CAREFUL TO PROTECT THE BRANDS THEY'VE CULTIVATED, AND THUS SHY AWAY FROM THE CONTROVERSY ASSOCIATED WITH ABORTION.

WHY SHOULD HOSPITALS, HEALTH SYSTEMS AND OTHER HEALTHCARE ORGANIZATIONS TAKE RESPONSIBILITY FOR PROVIDING ABORTION CARE?

TAX-EXEMPT STATUS OBLIGATES NONPROFIT ORGANIZATIONS TO ADDRESS THE COMMUNITY'S NEEDS

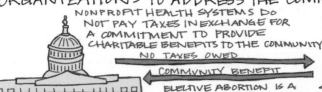

NONPROFIT HEALTH SYSTEMS DO NOT PAY TAXES IN EXCHANGE FOR A COMMITMENT TO PROVIDE CHARITABLE BENEFITS TO THE COMMUNITY

NONPROFIT HEALTH SYSTEM

NO TAXES OWED

COMMUNITY BENEFIT

FEDERAL GOVERNMENT

ELECTIVE ABORTION IS A COMMUNITY NEED AND IT IS WRONG FOR NONPROFIT HEALTH SYSTEMS TO IGNORE IT.

HEALTHCARE PROVIDERS HAVE UNIQUE RESPONSIBILITIES TO THEIR COMMUNITIES

WHETHER OPERATED FOR PROFIT OR NOT, HEALTHCARE ORGANIZATIONS ARE STEWARDS OF A COMMUNITY RESOURCE – HEALTH CARE – TO WHICH EVERY PERSON SHOULD BE AFFORDED EQUAL ACCESS. ABORTION CARE IS AN ESSENTIAL ELEMENT OF REPRODUCTIVE HEALTHCARE FOR PEOPLE CAPABLE OF BECOMING PREGNANT (JUST UNDER ½ OF THE POPULATION AT SOME POINT IN THEIR LIVES.)

HEALTHCARE ORGANIZATIONS CURRENTLY GET AWAY WITH PRETENDING THAT ABORTION ISN'T HEALTHCARE, OR THAT IT IS A CONVENIENCE RATHER THAN A BASIC NEED. THIS ATTITUDE PERSISTS DESPITE MOUNTING EVIDENCE THAT ABORTION ACCESS IS VITAL TO THE HEALTH AND WELFARE OF INDIVIDUALS AND COMMUNITIES.

POORER WOMEN'S HEALTH OUTCOMES

LEGAL ABORTION

CHILDBIRTH

RISK OF DEATH

WORSE ABORTION ACCESS

SOCIOECONOMIC DISADVANTAGES

IT IS TIME FOR HEALTH ORGANIZATIONS THAT FINANCIALLY THRIVE ON COMMUNITIES' ILLNESSES TO BE HELD ACCOUNTABLE FOR PROVIDING ALL OF THE BASIC CARE THE COMMUNITY NEEDS.

WE CAN START BY:

ADVOCATING FOR PUBLIC AND PRIVATE INSURANCE COVERAGE OF ABORTION

PROTESTING RELIGIOUS INFLUENCE OVER HEALTH CARE

INSISTING UPON EVIDENCE-BASED ABORTION EDUCATION IN HEALTH PROFESSIONS

DEMANDING THAT HEALTHCARE ORGANIZATIONS ADDRESS ABORTION AS A COMMUNITY HEALTH NEED

DISCUSSING ABORTION CARE WITH YOUR REGULAR HEALTHCARE PROVIDER

"Plan C"

Written by
Nomi Kane & the Plan C Team

Artwork by
Nomi Kane

Even with increased access to birth control, millions of people in the U.S. each year find themselves pregnant and don't want to be.

In 2006, Plan B (the morning after pill) became available over the counter in the U.S., providing another option for avoiding pregnancy...

Plan B One-Step

But, when Plan B fails, or is unavailable, folks need a "plan C". Fortunately, there is a safe, effective, F.D.A. approved solution for a missed period.

This "Plan C" is a combination of medications called mifepristone and misoprostol. When taken as directed up to 12 weeks after a missed period the pills are safe and 95% effective.

MIFEPRISTONE   MISOPROSTOL

In the U.S., the most common way to get mifepristone and misoprostol is from health care providers who offer abortion services...

But there are many barriers to access in the U.S. Because mifepristone and misoprostol enable people to safely and effectively manage early abortion on their own, some are obtaining and taking these pills independently.

Like many, you may prefer taking these pills on your own because it can be done in the comfort of your own home...

Because it affords privacy and avoids the potential stigma of going to a clinic...

Because it is less invasive than a surgical abortion...

Because it is generally less expensive than a surgical abortion...

Because it gives you more flexibility and does not require an appointment...

Nothing until the 21st?

Because it's your health, your body, and you should have the right to choose the option that is best for you.

In countries like Ghana and Mexico, abortion pills can be purchased easily and inexpensively at pharmacies.

And people in more than 100 countries have access to mail order services such as womenweb.org, womenhelp.org, and safe2choose.org.

But because of political controversy over abortion in our country, abortion clinics are closing, leaving people in some states with few options.

So, folks in the U.S. are finding ways to buy pills covertly online...

Or across the border in Mexico.

Some people are using misoprostol alone, which is roughly 85% effective. Misoprostol can be easier to find because it's prescribed for arthritis, peptic ulcers, and even for pets.

In many states, anti-choice activists are working hard to make all abortion, including self-use of these pills, illegal or heavily restricted...

#ANTICHOICE

However, pro-choice activists are fighting back!

PlanCpills.org can help you learn more about the safe and effective use of mifepristone and misoprostol...

As well as the legal implications of obtaining and using these medications outside of the medical system.

You can join the fight: Help spread the word about "Plan C" and advocate for better access to this safe and effective method.

KEEP YOUR LAWS OFF MY BODY

ACCESS NOW!

TRUST WOMEN.

©NOMI KANE '17

Visit www.PlanCpills.org to learn more.
*This is not a substitute for the representation of an attorney or the advice of a doctor.

I WANT MY BIRTH CONTROL TO LAST FOR THE ENTIRE TRUMP ADMINISTRATION—
IF THEY REPEAL OBAMACARE, MY BIRTH CONTROL COVERAGE WILL DISAPPEAR.
IUDS LAST FIVE TO TEN YEARS— HOPEFULLY LONGER THAN THE PRESIDENT'S TERM.

I AM FAR FROM ALONE WITH THIS FEAR

IN THE MONTH AFTER THE ELECTION, SOME PLANNED PARENTHOODS SAW A 400% INCREASE IN IUD APPOINTMENTS

I'VE NEVER WANTED TO BE PREGNANT

BUT I'VE ONLY BEEN ABLE TO MAKE THAT CHOICE THANKS TO LUCK AND PRIVILEGE

OUR LAWS & UNEQUAL SOCIETY MAKE IT ABSURDLY DIFFICULT TO CONTROL YOUR OWN REPRODUCTION.

TRUMP SIGNS A HISTORIC BILL TO CUT WOMEN'S HEALTH FUNDING.

HALF OF ALL PREGNANCIES IN THE UNITED STATES ARE UNPLANNED.

IT'S ALWAYS EASY TO TAKE AWAY PEOPLE'S RIGHTS IF YOU DEMONIZE THEM.

RENEE BRACEY SHERMAN
REPRODUCTIVE JUSTICE ACTIVIST

DEMONIZE THEM, DEHUMANIZE THEM, AND TAKE THEM OUT OF THE CONVERSATION.

NEXT HEALTH CLINIC: 500 MILES

FOR MANY PEOPLE— ESPECIALLY LOW INCOME PEOPLE & PEOPLE OF COLOR— THE CHALLENGES TO GETTING BIRTH CONTROL ARE BIG.

WITHOUT INSURANCE, GETTING AN IUD COSTS AN AVERAGE OF $1,600.

I THINK INVESTING IN FAMILY PLANNING IS THE SMARTEST INVESTMENT THE FEDERAL GOVERNMENT CAN MAKE.

CECILE RICHARDS

PRESIDENT OF THE PLANNED PARENTHOOD FEDERATION OF AMERICA

"I THINK THEY SHOULD BE JUST DROPPING IT OUT OF AIRPLANES AND IT SHOULD BE FREE FOR EVERY WOMAN."

IN 2009, COLORADO STARTED AN EXPERIMENT.

THE STATE OFFERED FREE LONG-LASTING BIRTH CONTROL — IUDs & IMPLANTS — TO TEENS AND LOW-INCOME WOMEN

OVER ITS SIX-YEAR TRIAL, THOUSANDS OF PEOPLE SIGNED UP FOR THE BIRTH-CONTROL PROGRAM.

THE RESULTS?

Go TEAM!

TEEN PREGNANCIES DECLINED 40%.

ABORTION RATES DECLINED 42%.

THE STATE SAVED $60 MILLION IN MEDICAID COSTS.

ONE OF THE SIMPLEST AND MOST EFFECTIVE WAYS TO REDUCE POVERTY IS TO MAKE SURE PEOPLE ONLY BECOME PARENTS WHEN THEY WANT TO.

THEN IN 2015, REPUBLICANS IN THE STATE LEGISLATURE REFUSED TO FUND THE PROGRAM.

"Unfortunately, family planning is a political issue and science and data gets trumped by an ideology."

—GRETA KLINGLER, COLORADO DEPT. OF PUBLIC HEALTH

"OCTOBER"

by kris louis

it was october 2012 when i found out that i was pregnant.

my boyfriend and i went to a convention, and the whole weekend i expected to get my period, but it never came.

at the time, i blamed my breast pain on the tight sports bras i wore before i started to use binders.

but...

but i'm on the pill...

you never think it can happen to you.

we went to planned parenthood to confirm
what we already knew.

okay, so...

the test
was
positive

so let's
discuss
your
options.

HA!
HAHA-

i'm getting an abortion. so tell me what i need to do next

all right. we can move forward with your next appointment

and in the meantime, look over these pamphlets, they'll give you an idea of all of your options between now and then.

thank you

i couldn't even consider a future where i had any other options.

this was all complicated by the fact that i had begun to wonder if i was transgender.

being pregnant was the most confusing thing that could have happened.

hey, mom.

good, um... so... hey...

SKTCH

i'm pregnant?

haha...

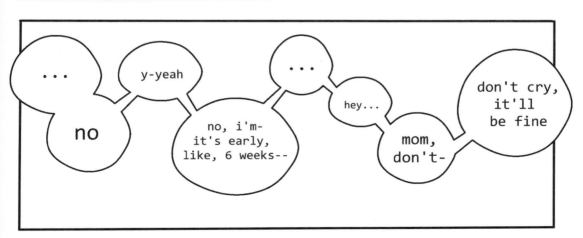

...

no

y-yeah

no, i'm- it's early, like, 6 weeks--

...

hey...

mom, don't-

don't cry, it'll be fine

the next few days were a blur. i went to my ob/gyn for an ultrasound

do you want to see it?

uh... sure

can you see? that little grey cloudy mass?

um...

oh in the top corner? it's... so small.

they gave me pills to put between my teeth and my gums and some painkillers.

it still hurt. it was like the most intense cramps i've ever had. i didn't throw up, but i spent the entire time in the bathroom, weeping and waiting for it to all be over.

the fact that I had extinguished a life was hard to think about, but at that point in my life...

every few days I thought about dying.

I was failing all of my classes. My hard drive crashed. My relationships were crumbling around me.

i was a mess.

TCH.

i don't want to sugarcoat it.
getting an abortion was one of
the hardest, loneliest
things i've ever done.
to pretend that it was easy or
convenient would be
a disservice to me
and others like me.

i think about the child
that could have been,
and the kind of life
i'd have given,
and i'm glad that their spirit
never had a chance
to fasten to that tiny
cloud of cells I couldn't quite see.

i'm glad i had the choice.

i only wish i wasn't so alone
for it all. there was no precedent
for me to draw on: as a young, confused
trans person, my own body had turned
against me. dysphoria was an under-
statement, i felt like an alien
at the whim of organs and blood
that had pinned me inside of them.
i was trapped under a wave of fate,
and when i chose to change it,

nobody was there to say

"it's ok."

"i see you."

"you're not alone."

but it's getting better.

i have a tribe now.

i am safe, loved, and wanted.

my friends had a baby and it's got me thinking.

one day, maybe.

until then, i'll grieve for the child that wasn't.

and i'll be glad that i had a choice.

MY BIRTH MOM GREW UP CATHOLIC. THE ONLY THING SHE WAS TOLD ABOUT SEX WAS "DON'T HAVE IT."

SHE GOT KNOCKED UP BY HER COLLEGE BOYFRIEND BECAUSE SHE DIDN'T KNOW WHAT A CONDOM WAS.

HE TOOK HER TO A PLANNED PARENTHOOD WITHOUT REALIZING MORE EXPLANATION WAS NEEDED. SHE WAS HORRIFIED.

SHE LEFT ALONE YELLING "THERE ARE OTHER OPTIONS" ON HER WAY OUT, THEN WALKED THREE HOURS HOME FROM DOWNTOWN CINCINNATI (A ROUGH PLACE IN THE LATE '80s).

OTHER OPTIONS BY ELIOT LADY

VOLVO

SPEED LIMIT 45

GROWING UP AS AN ADOPTED CHILD I HAD AN ACCUTE KNOWLEDGE THAT I HAD NEARLY BEEN ABORTED, AND IT GAVE ME AN UNEASY CLOSENESS TO THE SUBJECT.

I WAS NEVER REALLY ANTI-CHOICE, BUT I DEFINITELY DIDN'T LIKE THE IDEA OF ABORTION.

I HAD A PREGNANCY SCARE IN HIGH SCHOOL, AND MY MOM TOLD ME WE WERE GOING TO PLANNED PARENTHOOD FOR AN ABORTION, AND THAT I DIDN'T HAVE A CHOICE.

MY PERIOD CAME THE NEXT DAY, BUT THE TRAUMA HAD BEEN DONE.

TIME WENT ON - AS IT DOES - AND I REALIZED THAT OF COURSE I WOULD HAVE GOTTEN AN ABORTION HAD I BEEN GIVEN MY OWN TIME AND SPACE TO THINK ABOUT WHAT HAVING A CHILD WOULD MEAN.

THIS WAS REINFORCED WHEN I MET MY BIRTH MOM AT EIGHTEEN. PEOPLE TALK ABOUT HOW AN ABORTION AFFECTS YOU, BUT HAVING TO GIVE UP A CHILD STATISTICALLY HAS MUCH LONGER-LASTING PSYCHOLOGICAL RAMIFICATIONS.*

TODAY I'M A GENDERQUEER INDIVIDUAL WITH NO DESIRE FOR CHILDREN OF MY OWN, AND A STRONG BELIEF THAT PEOPLE SHOULD BE ALLOWED TO DECIDE WHAT SHAPE THEIR LIFE WILL TAKE. MAYBE I'LL EVEN DONATE MY EGGS TO A FRIEND WHO NEEDS THEM MORE THAN I DO.

WE FORGET JUST HOW MANY OPTIONS THERE ARE.
EVERY ONE OF THEM IS VALID.

MY NAME IS SAGE COFFEY AND I HAD AN ABORTION.

SUMMER 2016

HUFF HUFF

I DIDN'T TELL ANYONE.

I got to go to the bathroom NOW I'm soooo SORRY

NO ONE HAD TO KNOW.

AND WHEN THEY ASKED

BLYGGHH

ARE YOU OKAY?!

I LIED.

YEAH, I JUST GOT FOOD POISONING. I'M FINE.

I PARTIED TOO HARD LAST NIGHT, HAHAHA!

I THINK THERE'S A BUG GOING AROUND. IS YOUR THROAT SCRATCHY?

I JUST GOT MY PERIOD. CRAMPS CITY!!

I PULLED AN ALL-NIGHTER LAST NIGHT. FREELANCE LIFE!

THE FIRST ATTEMPT FAILED. MY EXCUSES GOT MORE ELABORATE TO COVER UP THE FACT THAT I MIGHT NEED SURGERY IF THE SECOND ATTEMPT AT A MEDICAL ABORTION FAILED. I DIDN'T WANT TO SEE OR TALK TO ANYONE.

I, UH, SWITCHED MEDICATION RECENTLY.

I'VE BEEN SO UNHEALTHY. I THINK I GOT AN ULCER!

THE DOCTOR SAID I DEVELOPED CYSTS FROM STRESS.

I MIGHT GET SURGERY TO REMOVE THOSE CYSTS. CAN YOU COVER MY SHIFT?

IF I HAD JUST TOLD SOMEONE

I WOULD'VE GOTTEN THE SUPPORT I DESPERATELY NEEDED.

SELF CARE AFTER YOUR ABORTION

BY RACHEL HAYS

AFTER YOUR ABORTION YOUR BODY WILL EXPERIENCE CHANGE AS IT RETURNS TO ITS NON-PREGNANT STATE.

CRAMPS CAN BE RELIEVED BY HEAT, ICE, AND DEEP UTERINE MASSAGE. MASSAGE IN A DOWNWARD MOTION FROM YOUR BELLY BUTTON TO YOUR PUBIC BONE. THIS HELPS PASS CLOTS.

LIGHT STRETCHING CAN ALSO HELP.

WARM LIQUIDS CAN BE COMFORTING. IBUPROFEN CAN HELP WITH POST-ABORTION CRAMPING. DON'T TAKE ASPIRIN, WHICH INCREASES BLEEDING.

BLEEDING AFTER ABORTION IS USUALLY DIFFERENT THAN A PERIOD. SOME PEOPLE PASS CLOTS, AND HAVE STRONG CRAMPING. ITS NORMAL TO STOP BLEEDING AND START AGAIN A FEW DAYS LATER, OR NOT TO BEGIN BLEEDING FOR SEVERAL DAYS AFTER THE ABORTION.

FOR AT LEAST ONE WEEK AFTER YOUR ABORTION DON'T PUT ANYTHING INTO YOUR VAGINA. USE PADS INSTEAD OF TAMPONS OR MENSTRUAL CUPS. DON'T HAVE VAGINAL SEX. YOUR CERVIX IS OPEN, AND SO THERE'S RISK OF INFECTION.

SOME DOCTORS RECOMMEND SHOWERS RATHER THAN BATHS FOR A FEW DAYS.

YOUR BREASTS HAVE ENLARGED TO PRODUCE MILK. THEY MIGHT FEEL SORE OR HARD. THEY MAY LEAK.
DON'T SQUEEZE OR STIMULATE THEM, WHICH WILL INCREASE LEAKAGE. ICE CAN HELP WITH PAIN.

SOME DOCTORS RECOMMEND LONG PERIODS OF REST. CHECK IN WITH YOUR BODY. COMPLICATIONS FROM ABORTION ARE RARE.
DO CALL YOUR DOCTOR IF YOU HAVE A FEVER, FAINTING OR PROLONGED HEAVY BLEEDING.

IT'S JUST AS IMPORTANT TO CHECK IN WITH YOUR MENTAL HEALTH AFTER YOUR ABORTION.

FEELINGS OF RELIEF, SADNESS, ELATION OR DEPRESSION ARE COMMON. THIS IS IN PART BECAUSE OF STRONG HORMONAL CHANGES THAT OCCUR AFTER YOUR ABORTION.

IT CAN BE HELPFUL TO DISCUSS THESE FEELINGS. THERE ARE MANY FREE POST-ABORTION COUNSELING SERVICES AS WELL AS SUPPORT GROUPS AND HELP LINES ALL OVER THE COUNTRY.

REACH OUT IF YOU FEEL LIKE YOU WANT TO TALK ABOUT YOUR ABORTION AND IF YOU DON'T KNOW THAT'S OK TOO.

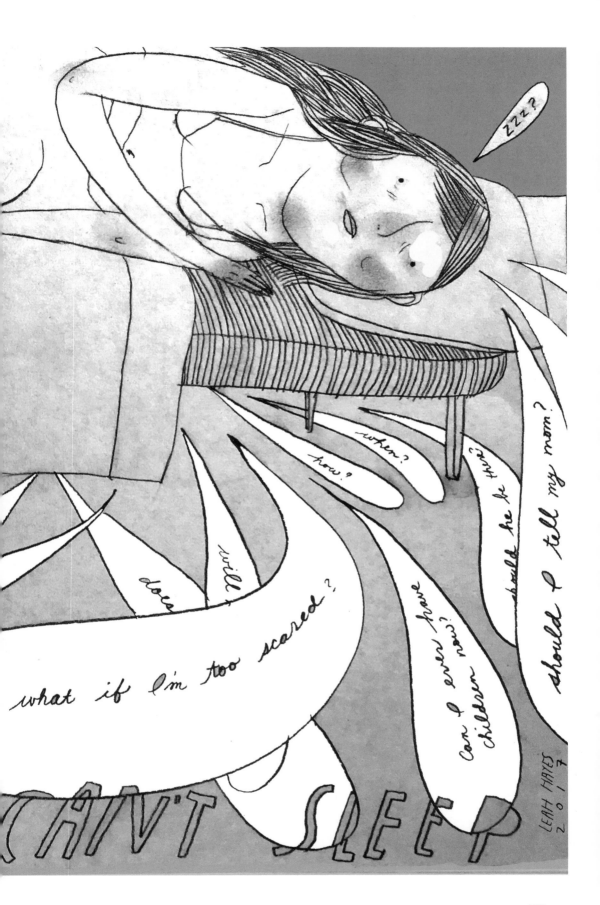

PAST TENSE, FUTURE FORWARD

WRITTEN BY TANYA DEPASS

ART BY WREN CHAVERS

ARE YOU SURE?

YES, POSITIVE RESULT I'M SORRY

THE LATE 1990S...

THANK YOU, I NEED A FEW MINUTES PLEASE

OF COURSE, I'LL HAVE INFORMATION FOR YOU WAITING AT THE DESK

I SHOULD HAVE KNOWN BETTER...

THAT PLACE SEEMED TOO GOOD TO BE TRUE

DON'T BLAME YOURSELF, LET'S TRY AGAIN TOMORROW

FOUND PLANNED PARENTHOOD

MIGHT AS WELL CALL FIRST TO BE SURE

THANK YOU

I'LL SEE YOU IN TWO WEEKS

WHAT IF WE'RE WRONG?

NOT WRONG,
WE MADE THE BEST DECISION
EVEN IF IT WASN'T AN EASY ONE.
REST UP, I'LL BE HERE

I...HOPE SO,
IT JUST REALLY
FUCKING HURTS.

WHY DO I FEEL SO BAD?

2016

ding!

WHY ARE PEOPLE TRYING TO ACT LIKE ABORTIONS ARE EASY BIRTH CONTROL? WHAT THE HELL?

Scroll ↓ Scroll

Now Trending:

#ShoutYourAbortion

Linda F @Sunriseluvr
#ShoutYourAbortion activists 4get th-

Paula448 @Paula448
#ShoutYourAbortion

USFamFriend @USFamFriend
#ShoutYourAbortion sounds like glo-

WHAT IS THIS BULLSHIT?

FROM PUBERTY ON, MY BIGGEST FEAR WAS GETTING PREGNANT.

MY PERIOD WAS NEVER REGULAR. I WASN'T EVEN HAVING SEX YET, BUT...

WHEN I WAS 16 I DID A LITTLE 'HEAVY PETTING' AND DIDN'T GET MY PERIOD FOR MONTHS AFTER.

PLEASE GOD*

STILL NOTHING

DON'T LET ME BE PREGNANT!

*DIDN'T BELIEVE IN GOD – WAS PRAYING ANYWAYS!

I FELT TRAPPED. EVEN WITH LIBERAL PARENTS THERE WAS **NO WAY** I WAS MENTIONING IT TO THEM.

$20!!! I DON'T HAVE $20!

EPT

PREGNANCY TEST-$20

OTHER TEST-$40

THANKFULLY A FRIEND TOLD ME TO TRY PLANNED PARENTHOOD

YOUR TEST SHOWS YOU'RE NOT PREGNANT

AND, THERE'S NO CHARGE

THANK YOU!

OVER THE NEXT DOZEN YEARS I HAD OTHER SCARES. MANY EPT'S WERE USED. MY PERIOD STILL ONLY SHOWED UP A FEW TIMES A YEAR.

not pregnant

THANK GOD!

ANOTHER DAY, ANOTHER SCARE. IN AUGUST 2001 I WAS SURE I WAS PREGNANT. I GOT TESTED BY MY DOCTOR AND IT WAS NEGATIVE.

WOOHOO IF THERE IS ONE THING I'M NOT IT'S PREGNANT!

GOOD, BECAUSE IF I WAS, I WOULD RUN, NOT WALK, TO THE ABORTION CLINIC!

UNBEKNOWNST TO ME, I GOT PREGNANT NOT A WEEK LATER.

SOON AFTER THAT I WENT TO BURNING MAN AND PARTIED DOWN

BINGE DRINKING
DEHYDRATION
ECSTACY
CHAIN SMOKING
CRYSTAL METH
NITROUS
MED TENT

I FEARED FOR MY LIFE AND WAS UNUSUALLY VIGILANT ABOUT EXTERNAL THREATS

ARE YOU THREATENING ME?!*

*USUALLY FINE WITH BEING THREATENED

I WAS RELIGIOUS* ABOUT USING BIRTH CONTROL. AFTER THE PILL MADE ME DEPRESSED I USED A DIAPHRAGM & SPERMICIDE.

*NO PUN INTENDED

SPERM-X

THE EFFECTIVENESS SOUNDED GOOD ENOUGH, IN RETROSPECT THEY WERE NOT!

I CAME HOME FROM BURNING MAN AND HAD A 4-MONTH LONG BREAKDOWN. I WENT BACK TO MY DOCTOR AGAIN AND AGAIN.

I'M GOING INSAAANE!

HMM, HERE'S AN RX FOR WELLBUTRIN AND A REFERRAL FOR A PSYCHIATRIST.

I WAS HAVING CONSTANT PANIC ATTACKS AND PRACTICALLY HALLUCINATING WITH PARANOIA. MY BOOBS KEPT HAVING STABBING PAINS.

YOU ALL HATE ME!

TATS, NO! WE ALL LOVE YOU!

I SUSPECTED I MIGHT BE PREGNANT - BUT THEN I HAD WHAT LOOKED LIKE MY PERIOD.

PHEW! IF YOU BLEED OUT YOUR VAG IT MEANS YOU'RE NOT PREGNANT!

NOT TRUE!

EVENTUALLY MY DOC TOOK BLOOD SAMPLES TO CHECK FOR THYROID, ETC. ISSUES.

EVEN THOUGH WE TESTED FOR PREGNANCY ALREADY, LET'S TEST AGAIN WHILE WE'RE AT IT.

SOON AFTER MY DOC CALLED WITH THE NEWS... I WAS VERY PREGNANT.

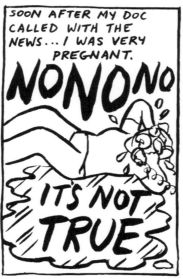

NONONO

IT'S NOT TRUE

I WAS ALREADY LOSING IT AND THE NOTION THERE WAS AN UNINVITED PARASITE INSIDE ME FELT RIGHT OUT OF THE MOVIE "ALIEN"

AAAA GET IT OUT!

A FRIEND CAME WITH ME TO THE ULTRASOUND. I SUSPECT THE TECHNICIAN WAS PRO-LIFE.

LOOK AT IT! HERE YOU CAN SEE ITS TINY LITTLE HANDS AND OOH! I CAN SEE ITS HEART BEATING!

WAAAAAAAA

I SAW MY DOC TO DISCUSS MY OPTIONS. I WAS FOUR MONTHS ALONG. I SUSPECT MY DOC WAS PRO-LIFE.

OH, I'M GETTING AN ABORTION.

OR, YOU COULD KEEP IT! OR PUT IT UP FOR ADOPTION!

NO.

BUT...

SHE LEFT THE ROOM SO I COULD 'CONSIDER'- I GRABBED HER PHONE AND CALLED CLINICS UNTIL I FOUND ONE THAT WOULD TAKE ME IN MY SECOND TRIMESTER

IT COSTS HOW MUCH?

I DON'T HAVE ANY MONEY!

IT COST THOUSANDS OF DOLLARS UP FRONT, NO COVERAGE! LUCKILY I QUALIFIED FOR ASSISTANCE.

AT FOUR MONTHS, I NEEDED A 'D&E'-DILATION AND EVACUATION. NO CLINICS IN LIBERAL SEATTLE WOULD DO IT. I FOUND ONE ON THE OUTSKIRTS OF TOWN, IN THE RED LIGHT DISTRICT.

THAT NIGHT, AS I WAS LOSING MY SHIT, MY BOYFRIEND AND I HAD A MATURE DISCUSSION ABOUT THE SITUATION.

THIS IS ALL YOUR FAULT!

WHAT?! THIS IS ALL YOUR FAULT!

THE NEXT FEW DAYS D R A G G E D PAST AS I WAITED FOR MY APPOINTMENTS. AT WORK MY BOSS SENT ME HOME - ONE LOOK AND HE KNEW I WASN'T WELL.

A FRIEND DROVE ME OUT TO THE BOONIES FOR MY DIALATION APPOINTMENT. I HAD A MANDATORY COUNSELING TO MAKE SURE I WAS SURE.

NOW...

I'M SURE.

WELL...

I'M SURE

I WOULDN'T LIVE THROUGH 5 MORE MONTHS OF PREGNANCY AND I'M SURE I'D BRAIN DAMAGED THE FETUS.

IT WAS THE LONGEST WAIT OF MY LIFE

DILATION=INSERTING OSMOTIC METAL RODS INTO MY CERVIX. THEY WOULD EXPAND OVERNIGHT TO DILATE MY CERVIX

AHHHHG

I WENT HOME AND WAITED AS THE RODS EXPANDED. FRIENDS CAME BY FOR MORAL SUPPORT. I TOOK PAINKILLERS BUT THEY BARELY MADE A DENT

AAGHKHH

THE NEXT DAY MY BOYFRIEND DROVE ME BACK OUT FOR MY EVACUATION. ANOTHER INFINITE WAIT.

Scraping & sucking

IT WAS HORRIBLE BUT THE DRUGS WERE INCREDIBLE. I FLOATED IN THE CLOUDS PAINTED ON THE CEILING

A FEW DAYS LATER I CAME HOME FROM WORK AND REALIZED I'D BEEN LACTATING

AIEEEE

INTERNALIZED MISOGYNY

SEX ISSUES

MOMMY ISSUES

BODY ISSUES

IN 2001 (AGE 26) NONE OF MY FRIENDS HAD KIDS YET. I DIDN'T KNOW ANYONE WHO'D HAD AN ABORTION WHO'D TOLD ME. I DIDN'T USE THE INTERNET A TON. I THOUGHT I WAS ONE IN A MILLION

SHAME
FALLEN WOMAN
URBAN LEGENDS ABOUT GIRLS WHO DON'T KNOW THEY'RE PREGNANT
FUCKUP WHO CAN'T USE BIRTH CONTROL RIGHT!

I DIDN'T KNOW ANYONE WHO'D MISCARRIED. I DIDN'T KNOW WHAT WAS HAPPENING TO MY BODY.

LOSS
GRIEF
CONFUSION
ANXIETY
DEPRESSION
IMBALANCE
CRAZED FROM HORMONES

in your place an empty space

I SWALLOWED IT. I HAD NOWHERE TO PUT THESE EMOTIONS, AND ONE GO-TO SKILL SET FOR PAIN MANAGEMENT.

booze pot pills coke NO₂

THE LITTLE FAITH I HAD IN LIFE WAS GONE. I NEVER IMAGINED THINGS COULD FEEL SO AWFUL AND DARK.

A FEW MONTHS LATER, I DREW A COMIC ABOUT MY ABORTION.

I COULD NEVER PUBLISH THIS!

HM, WELL MAYBE ONE DAY, IF IT WAS ANONYMOUS.

OR I'LL BURY IT IN A BOX AND NEVER LOOK AT IT AGAIN! (WHAT I DID, FOR 13 YEARS!)

OVER THE NEXT FEW YEARS I BECAME MORE ACTIVE ONLINE AND NOTICED A FEW WOMEN MENTION THEY'D HAD ABORTIONS. I STILL ASSUMED I WAS ONE OF THE FEW. I CHEERED FOR PRO-CHOICE BUT NEVER GOT INVOLVED

WOW SHE TALKS ABOUT BEING PRO-CHOICE RIGHT ON HER BLOG...COOL!

OK I'LL SIGN THE NARAL E-PETITION

EVERY TIME I STOPPED DRINKING, ESPECIALLY WHEN I QUIT FOR GOOD IN 2009, MY ABORTION SHAME EMERGED.

I'VE ALWAYS BEEN PRO-CHOICE

WHY DO I FEEL THIS WAY?

MURDERER

BABY KILLER

IN 2014 I DUG OUT THE COMIC I'D DRAWN OF MY ABORTION. I SHARED IT SELECTIVELY. IT BROUGHT UP SO MUCH GRIEF I WAS CRAWLING ON ALL FOURS.

DON'T TALK ABOUT IT

IF I'D KEPT IT, IT WOULD BE 13 YEARS OLD! AND BRAIN DAMAGED. AND I'D BE DEAD OR LOCKED UP...

IN 2015 I DISCOVERED THE SHOUT YOUR ABORTION MOVEMENT. SO. MANY. WOMEN WERE SHARING THEIR STORY! I LEARNED ONE IN FOUR WOMEN HAD AN ABORTION! SINCE NO ONE TALKED ABOUT IT, I HAD ASSUMED IT WAS RARE AND SHAMEFUL.

I'M... I'M... NORMAL?

PEOPLE ARE TALKING ABOUT THEIR ABORTIONS ON FACEBOOK!? WE CAN DO THAT?

IN 2016 I WENT TO A SHOUT YOUR ABORTION RALLY. I SAW PEOPLE THERE FROM MY DAY-TO-DAY LIFE. I STOOD IN A CROWD AS WE CELEBRATED OUR CHOICES AND SOLIDARITY. I WEPT WITH RELIEF.

I DON'T HAVE TO BE ASHAMED

I FELT LIKE 1,000 TONS WERE LIFTED OFF ME AND HAVEN'T FELT THE SHAME SINCE.

I WEAR THE SHIRT I GOT AT THE S.Y.A. RALLY TO OTHER EVENTS AND MARCHES - WITH PRIDE.

EVERYONE KNOWS I HAD AN ABORTION

WOMEN HAVE RUN UP TO ME AND HUGGED ME FOR IT.

THANK YOU FOR WEARING THAT SHIRT!

I HAD ONE, TOO.

AW THANK YOU!

LIVING A RELATIVELY PRIVILEGED LIFE, THE THOUGHTS AND FEELINGS I HAD AROUND MY PREGNANCY AND ABORTION WAS THE WORST THING TO EVER HAPPEN TO ME.

I HAVE NEVER FELT THIS BAD

THIS AFRAID

THIS ASHAMED

THIS ROTTEN

I NEVER KNEW ANYONE COULD FEEL THIS BAD

THIS FUCKED OVER

THIS WRONG

THIS DARK

MY SOUL

I DIDN'T THINK ABORTION WAS WRONG, BUT I FELT SO BAD I REASONED I MUST BE BAD.

AS I GOT OLDER, MANY FRIENDS GOT PREGNANT AND FRIENDS LOST EMBRYOS FOR A VARIETY OF REASONS.

YOU MISCARRIED AND NOW YOU HAVE TO GET THE FETUS VACCUMED OUT? I'M SO SORRY! OH HON, THAT SOUNDS SO TRAUMATIC. ♡

HUH... MAYBE WHAT I WENT THROUGH WAS TRAUMATIC*!

*I IMAGINE CHILDBIRTH AND RAISING KIDS CAN ALSO BE TRAUMATIC!

MY FRIEND HAS BEEN SO DEPRESSED AND DEVASTATED SINCE SHE MISCARRIED. IT MAKES SENSE BIOLOGICALLY!

EVEN THOUGH I CHOSE TO HAVE AN ABORTION, MY BODY MAY HAVE STILL BEEN REALLY UPSET THAT IT 'LOST' A PREGNANCY!

I NEVER PROCESSED MY GRIEF IN A HEALTHY, CATHARTIC WAY. I BEAT MYSELF UP FOR BEING A HUMAN!

I STARTED TO SEE FIRSTHAND HOW PREGNANCY CAN AFFECT SOMEONE.

ARE YOU FUCKING WITH ME?!

BAWS

I JUST NEED A FEW MORE NAPS

OHH... OF COURSE I WAS LOSING IT!

I AM STUNNED THAT DESPITE BEING RAISED IN LIBERAL SEATTLE AND IDENTIFYING AS PRO-CHOICE, I DID NOT FIND A COMMUNITY WILLING TO ADMIT TO AND DISCUSS THEIR ABORTIONS UNTIL I WAS 40 YEARS OLD!

I'M GLAD I MADE THE CHOICE I DID!

ME TOO!

LATELY I'VE SEEN ZINES, ARTICLES, COMICS AND BOOKS WHERE PEOPLE TALK ABOUT THEIR ABORTIONS. I NOW HAVE A COLLECTION!

Shrill

Dear Doctor ♡

GREY AREA

SHOUT YOUR ABORTION NYC

I HAD AN ABORTION AND IT WAS FINE

LOUDER

MANY OF THEM SAY THAT IT WAS NOT HARD, SHAMEFUL OR REGRETTABLE - ESPECIALLY ONES THAT HAPPENED IN A POST-SECRETIVE WORLD.

HAPPY OR SAD, EASY OR HARD, EARLY OR LATE TERM, HAVING AN ABORTION IS OKAY.

IT IS YOUR ABORTION. YOU GET TO TALK ABOUT IT. THIS SHOUT YOUR ABORTION SLOGAN SUMS IT UP:

OUR STORIES ARE OURS TO TELL.

THIS IS MINE.

Bearing Witness
LIFE AS AN ABORTION DOULA
BY MICK MORAN

AN ABORTION DOULA IS SOMEONE WHO PROVIDES *physical, emotional, & informational support* BEFORE, DURING, AND/OR AFTER AN ABORTION PROCEDURE. THAT CAN MEAN HOLDING THEIR HAND, TALKING TO THEM ABOUT BIRTH CONTROL, DOING BREATHING EXERCISES, AND MORE. SOMETIMES THIS ROLE IS FILLED BY A NURSE, SOCIAL WORKER, OR FRIEND, BUT SOME CLINICS HAVE A SPECIFIC ABORTION DOULA ROLE. I'm an abortion doula.

HOLDING SPACE

WE TALK A LOT IN OUR WORK ABOUT "HOLDING SPACE." THIS CONCEPT CAN BE HARD TO EXPLAIN. FOR ME, SOME OF THE THINGS IT ENCOMPASSES ARE:

OFFERING *unconditional ~ support ~* THROUGH LISTENING, KIND WORDS, OR TOUCH

REMEMBERING IT'S NOT ABOUT ME

witnessing THEIR EXPERIENCES IN A WAY THAT MAKES THEM FEEL *Seen + heard*

AVOID TRYING TO FIX THINGS -or- *offer advice,* UNLESS I'M ASKED

GIVING THEM A SAFE SPACE TO FEEL *their* FEELINGS

TRUSTING + EMPOWERING THEM, SUPPORTING *Self-advocacy* INSTEAD OF ADVOCATING FOR THEM, AND NEVER SUBSTITUTING MY JUDGMENT FOR THEIRS.

MY ABORTION DOULA WORK DOES NOT JUST EXIST INSIDE THESE DOORS

CLINIC

I TALK OPENLY ABOUT MY WORK AS AN ABORTION DOULA, AND I FIND MYSELF HOLDING SPACE FOR PEOPLE IN UNUSUAL PLACES. SOMEONE I MEET AT A PARTY MIGHT SHARE THEIR STORY OF BIRTH, ABORTION, OR LOSS. SOMETIMES THEY HAVE FELT SUCH STIGMA THAT THEY HAVE NEVER SHARED THE STORY BEFORE.

I ALSO HEAR MANY STORIES WHILE AT EVENTS WITH OUR ZINE ABOUT ABORTION SELF-CARE.

I WISH I HAD THIS WHEN I HAD MY abortion

i've HAD this EXPERIENCE

I'M VERKLEMPT

My best friend NEEDS THIS RIGHT NOW I CAN'T BELIEVE I MET YOU TODAY. I'M SENDING THIS TO HER. I just got Chills.

SELF-CARE FOR ABORTION

ZINE

Because she had AN ACCENT, THE PROVIDER DIDN'T EXPLAIN EVERYTHING TO HER. SHE'S STILL SCARED AND GUILTY BECAUSE THEY DIDN'T GIVE HER GOOD CARE OR INFORMATION. maybe this will help.

BUT I HEAR FROM A LOT OF SUPPORT PEOPLE, TOO.

I'M NOT ALWAYS SURE HOW PEOPLE WILL REACT WHEN I TELL THEM ABOUT MY WORK BECAUSE OF THE STIGMA SURROUNDING ABORTION...

BUT PEOPLE OFTEN OVERWHELM ME WITH SUPPORT. THEIR REACTIONS, EVEN THE SILENT MOMENTS, CAN SHARE A STORY ABOUT ABORTION OR LOSS, SOMETIMES WITHOUT A SINGLE WORD BEING SPOKEN.

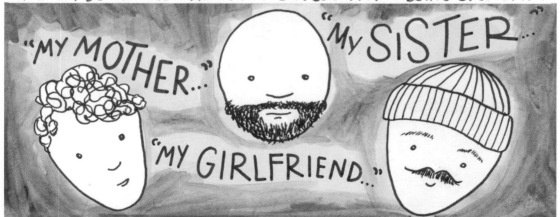

AND SOMETIMES I HEAR FROM ANOTHER GROUP. THEY OFTEN SPEAK ABOUT ABORTION IN A MORE HESITANT, UNCERTAIN WAY.

The STORIES PEOPLE SHARE about ABORTION, aren't always

EVEN IN THE CLINIC. SOMETIMES PEOPLE MIGHT BE PROCESSING A LONG-AGO SEXUAL ASSAULT OR ANOTHER TRAUMA. SOMETIMES THEY SHARE DIFFICULT CIRCUMSTANCES THAT THEY ARE FACING THAT CONTRIBUTE TO THEIR DECISION TO HAVE AN ABORTION. HOLDING SPACE IN ALL OF THESE SITUATIONS HAS MADE IT EASY FOR ME TO OFFER THAT SAME SUPPORT TO PEOPLE OUT IN THE WORLD, FRIENDS OR STRANGERS.

I have **HELD SPACE** for strangers on TRAINS, in CHURCHES, & in HOSPITALS.

I've been asked...

HOW HAS THIS WORK CHANGED YOU?

I HAVE PROBABLY HUGGED more strangers SINCE BECOMING A DOULA THAN EVER BEFORE IN MY LIFE. BEFORE, I MIGHT HAVE BEEN AFRAID TO INTRUDE IF I SAW SOMEONE STRUGGLING. NOW, I'LL OFFER WATER OR A HUG OR WHATEVER SUPPORT THEY SEEM TO NEED IN THE MOMENT.

PEOPLE rarely TURN DOWN THE HUG

WHETHER YOU SEE ME HOLDING A MICROPHONE WHILE SPEAKING ON A PANEL, HOLDING A COCKTAIL AT A PARTY, OR HOLDING SOMEONE'S BABY WHILE CHATTING ABOUT REPRODUCTIVE JUSTICE AT AN EVENT...

MY HEART IS OPEN. I SEE YOU. I HEAR YOU. YOU ARE NOT ALONE.

When It's Just A Job

I don't think 'pro-life' versus 'pro-choice' is a fair dichotomy when it comes to abortions.

PROLIFE

PROCHOICE

Have you been in a room where an abortion is taking place? It's full of life.

The doctors.

The nurses.

The patient.

The fetus.

And at times me (or another abortion doula).

me →

Written anonymously by an abortion doula   Art by Archie Bongiovanni

I don't think separating abortion from life is realistic or right, what we are doing is choosing life— the person who is pregnant.

I believe in autonomy for folks to choose what is best for them, I want to support them through this choice.

I've been an abortion doula for three years. Sometimes I'm there for the whole process, sometimes just part of it.

They are going to take your blood pressure next.

I can explain what the doctors are doing, I can hold their hand or rub their back. Sometimes I can just be a warm presence in an otherwise cold and calculated room.

Doulas are there to help and assist the patients.

People assume doctors and nurses are there to assist the patients but if you perform procedure after procedure eventually this becomes just a job.

I have seen enough rude, impatient, and frankly harmful medical staff to know that this is true.

I've seen nurses gossiping and laughing while my patient threw up over and over while she was still naked from the waist down and lightly bleeding from after the procedure.

The nurse just handed her a bin and left while I held her hair, fanned her, put a cool wet paper towel on her neck and tried to comfort her.

I've seen the pregnancy tissue left uncovered while the patient specifically said they don't want to see anything.

I have seen the procedure performed by med students who are required to learn how to do the procedure but have no interest in reproductive health care with no gentleness to patients.

I don't want to gloss over these harsh details because they are what many people face when they get the procedure done.

I also don't want to pretend that having an abortion doula present is going to make everything better (although we are useful in many instances).

Once I helped a woman whose language neither I nor the doctors spoke, I wasn't able to communicate with her or help her. The doctors couldn't communicate with her.

She was scared. I felt helpless to help her.

I love being an abortion doula but I am frustrated.

I am frustrated at doctors and nurses. I am frustrated at the pro-choice movement for dumbing these internal issues down.

As a genderqueer individual, I am frustrated at how gendered the movement is. I am frustrated at society that keeps policing people's bodies and choices, that we have to rationalize WHY we are choosing abortions.

I'm frustrated at an imperfect society full of stigma and judgement. I want to destigmatize and normalize abortions as much as possible.

But that's why I continue to do this work.

And I know that's why so many doctors continue their work too. I'm happy they are there, it's an important job, I just wish there was a bit more compassion all around.

mundoferpecto

WRITTEN BY: DANIELA DIAZ

DRAWN BY: STEPHANIE RODRIGUEZ

AT 29 I MOVED FROM PENNSYLVANIA TO D.C. I LEFT TO WORK AT A WOMEN'S REPRODUCTIVE HEALTH ORGANIZATION

AT THE TIME I WAS USING THE NUVA RING. I LIKED IT BECAUSE I DIDN'T HAVE TO TAKE A PILL EVERY DAY

AFTER 3 WEEKS OF WEARING THE NUVA RING I REMOVED IT AND WAITED FOR MY PERIOD TO BEGIN; BUT IT NEVER CAME.

WEIRD THINGS STARTED HAPPENING

I WAS FALLING ASLEEP AT WORK

MY CRAVINGS WERE OUT OF CONTROL!

ALL I WANT IS FRUIT

UGH

AND I HAD NAUSEA, BUT AT THE TIME I THOUGHT IT WAS ACID REFLUX.

6 DAYS PASSED; THE ANXIETY OF WAITING FOR MY PERIOD DROVE ME TO BUY A PREGNANCY TEST.

I WENT TO THE MARKET AND I BOUGHT $60 WORTH OF FRUIT AND PREGNANCY TESTS

LATER THAT DAY I TOOK THE TEST

HUH? WHERE'S THE CONTROL LINE?

I LEFT THE BATHROOM AND ATE SOME HONEYDEW MELON

THEN I CALLED MY FRIEND RACHEL FOR MORAL SUPPORT.

SO I TOOK OUT THE NUVARING AND IT WAS HARD TO REMOVE. I HAVEN'T GOTTEN MY PERIOD.

NOT LIKE THIS. NOT RIGHT NOW.

GULP!
HAHAHA

NERVOUS LAUGH

I BURST INTO WHAT I CALL THE MIDNIGHT GIGGLES

I LAUGHED BECAUSE I DID'NT FEEL FEAR; I LAUGHED BECAUSE I WAS IN A COUNTRY WHERE I HAD OPTIONS AND HAD THE LUCK OF BEING SURROUNDED BY PROFESSIONALS THAT WORK IN ABORTION.

AFTER RECEIVING THE RESULTS I CALLED MY NURSE PRACTITIONER FRIEND EMMA.

I WAS PRIVILEGED IN THAT I WORKED FOR A WOMEN'S REPRODUCTIVE ORGANIZATION. I KNEW MY RIGHTS, MY OPTIONS AND I COULD CONSULT WITH A PROFESSIONAL WORKING IN ABORTION.

MY EXPERIENCE IN THIS FIELD ALSO GAVE ME THE CONFIDENCE TO MAKE A POSITIVE DECISION WITHOUT ANY SHAME OR SELF BLAME.

BUT IT WASN'T ALL EASY.

A SNOWSTORM ROLLED INTO D.C. THE NIGHT BEFORE MY PROCEDURE.

THE CANCELLATION OF MY APPOINTMENT THREW ME INTO A FULL BLOWN PANIC ATTACK.

RESPIRA PROFUNDO

I HELD A LAVENDER PILLOW TO MY NOSE TO CALM MY NERVES

I DECIDED TO CALL MY MOM

¡MAMI TE NECESITO!

¡QUE TE PASO!

¡QUIEN TE MANDA NO USAR CONDON!

I PLANNED TO TELL MY FAMILY ABOUT THE ABORTION AFTER THE PROCEDURE. I WAS EXPECTING MY MOTHERS REACTION TO BE LIKE...

BUT THAT WASN'T THE CASE

¿COMO TE SIENTES?

ESTE FIN DE SEMANA TOMÉ UNA PRUEBA DE EMBARAZO Y SALIO POSITIVA. I MADE AN APPOINTMENT TO HAVE AN ABORTION Y LO CANCELARON BECAUSE OF THE SNOW STORM. **I'M SO STRESSED!**

MY MOM DECIDED TO COME DOWN TO D.C. TO SUPPORT ME DURING THE NEW PROCEDURE DATE.

PROCEDURE DAY

ON OUR WAY TO THE CLINIC I REALIZED THE CLINIC WAS BLOCKED BY PROTESTERS. I COULDN'T DEAL WITH THE STRESS OF THE PROCEDURE, PROTESTERS AND MY MOTHER'S NERVES.

I DECIDED IT WAS BEST FOR MY MOM NOT TO GO IN WITH ME.

GRACIAS MAMI. ¡TE QUIERO MUCHO!

NO TE PREOCUPES. ESTARÉ AQUÍ CUANDO SALGAS.

AS I WALKED INTO THE CLINIC I THOUGHT TO MYSELF.

= I'M CONFIDENT ABOUT MY DECISION =

AFTER THE PROCEDURE I HAD A FEELING OF EUPHORIA AND SADNESS. I WAS HAPPY.

I NEVER QUESTIONED MY DECISION BUT I HAD THOUGHTS ABOUT WHAT WOULD IT LOOK LIKE IF I KEPT IT. IT MADE ME SAD. I KNEW I WOULD HAVE STRUGGLED GREATLY.

¿COMO TE SIENTES?

ME SIENTO ¡LIBRE!

Most mornings I hit the snooze alarm four or five times before I get up. I always have.

Story: Renee Bracey Sherman
Art: Kennedy Tarrell

5:45

BUTTERFLIES

But one morning, ten years ago, I didn't sleep in. I couldn't.

BLEGH

I did everything right.

These things don't happen to girls like me.

What exactly do you WEAR to your abortion?

I decided the standard jeans and a t-shirt were good enough. Comfortable. Simple.

I learned I was pregnant the week before.

Haha, dude, she's SO TIRED. Your girlfriend's totally pregnant.

haha...

ha...

It all made sense. The nausea. The fatigue. The swelling of my breasts.

I bolted.

I discussed it with my boyfriend. Neither of us were ready to be parents.

LATER

I can't go with you. You're killing a piece of us.

It was then that I realized— This was the moment to finally put my needs and future first.

CLINIC PARKING

◦REC

SECURITY CAMERAS IN

BZZZZ

It's...

$350. That's how much my abortion cost. I couldn't use my insurance because my parents would find out. I hadn't told them. I figured I would one day. Just not today.

Years later, I would tell her.

I'm sorry, I was afraid you wouldn't love me. I was afraid you'd think I was a failure.

I'm so proud of you.

Honey, you didn't let me down.

You made the best decision for you.

I am so proud to be your mother. Never forget that.

BUT FOR NOW, I WAS ALONE.

Renee?

The nurse was orthodox Jewish. I'd thought all religious people hated people who have abortions.

Her smile was warm and genuine. I trusted her.

Now when I say my abortion was amazing, I'm not kidding.

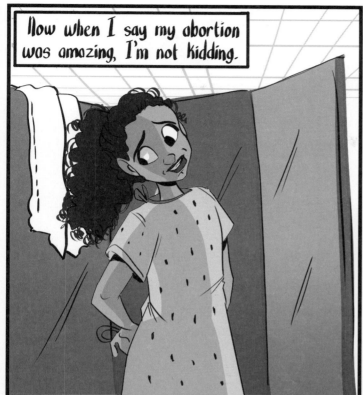

In TV and media, they talk about abortion providers as if they're evil. But that's just propaganda. Mine wasn't like that at all.

My doctor was caring. He made me smile.

Hellloooo, Renee!!!

And he looked curiously like Chef from South Park.

I hope that one day I get to meet him again and thank him.

Can you count back from 10 for me, Renee?

Her hands were soft. I imagine that's how my mom cared for her patients.

10...9...

She would have cared for me if she was here.

8...

7...6...

There were photos of butterflies taped to the ceiling. As I counted...

...I felt them fluttering.

They felt like... something new. Something reborn.

Like the moment I transformed my life. **Like love.**

ELEVEN

IN MEMORIAM

PEOPLE MURDERED
IN AMERICA
BY SO-CALLED
"PRO-LIFE" KILLERS

WORDS: JENNIFER CAMPER
ART: KATIE FRICAS

DAVID GUNN

DR. DAVID GUNN
NOVEMBER 16, 1945 –
MARCH 10, 1993

A DOCTOR WHO
PROVIDED ABORTIONS
AND WAS THREATENED
REPEATEDLY.
A DIVORCED FATHER
OF TWO. HIS DEATH
INSPIRED A MARILYN
MANSON SONG. SHOT
OUTSIDE THE CLINIC
IN PENSACOLA,
FLORIDA.

JOHN BAYARD BRITTON

DR. JOHN BAYARD
BRITTON
MAY 6, 1925 –
JULY 29, 1994

A DOCTOR WHO
PROVIDED ABORTIONS
AFTER DR. GUNN'S
DEATH. THOUGH HE
WAS AMBIVALENT
ABOUT THE
PROCEDURE, HE
NEEDED THE MONEY.
HE WAS THREATENED
OFTEN, WORE A
BULLET-PROOF
VEST, AND CARRIED
A GUN. SHOT IN HIS
TRUCK OUTSIDE THE
CLINIC IN PENSACOLA,
FLORIDA.

JAMES H. BARRETT

JAMES H. BARRETT
AUGUST 9, 1919 –
JULY 29, 1994

A RETIRED AIR FORCE
LT. COLONEL WHO
VOLUNTEERED AS A
SECURITY ESCORT
FOR DR. BRITTON. HE
WAS ACTIVE IN HIS
CHURCH AND MANY
COMMUNITY GROUPS.
HE WAS KILLED
WHILE ESCORTING
DR. BRITTON. HIS
WIFE, JUNE, ALSO
AN ESCORT, WAS
WOUNDED IN THE
SAME SHOOTING IN
PENSACOLA, FLORIDA.

SHANNON LOWNEY

SHANNON LOWNEY
JULY 7, 1969 –
DECEMBER 30, 1994

A RECEPTIONIST AT
PLANNED PARENTHOOD,
SHE HAD STUDIED IN
SPAIN AND WORKED
IN ECUADOR AS A
TRANSLATOR. SHE WAS
RAISED CATHOLIC,
BELIEVED STRONGLY IN
WOMEN'S HEALTH, AND
WAS PLANNING TO GET
HER MASTER'S DEGREE
IN SOCIAL WORK. SHOT
AT WORK IN BROOKLINE,
MASSACHUSETTS.

LEE ANN NICHOLS

LEE ANN NICHOLS
OCTOBER 27, 1956 –
DECEMBER 30, 1994

A RECEPTIONIST
AT PLANNED
PARENTHOOD,
ENGAGED TO BE
MARRIED. SHE WAS
RENOVATING HER
HOUSE WITH HER
FIANCÉ. SHE LOVED
NATURE AND HER
PETS. SHOT AT
WORK IN BROOKLINE,
MASSACHUSETTS.

ROBERT SANDERSON

ROBERT SANDERSON
JUNE 19, 1963 -
JANUARY 29, 1998

AN OFF-DUTY POLICE OFFICER WORKING AS A SECURITY GUARD AT A HEALTH CLINIC. MARRIED, WITH TWO STEP-CHILDREN, HE HAD SERVED IN THE AIR FORCE. HE WAS KILLED IN A BOMB EXPLOSION AT THE CLINIC IN BIRMINGHAM, ALABAMA. THE BOMB HAD BEEN SET BY THE SAME MAN WHO BOMBED THE ATLANTA CENTENNIAL OLYMPIC PARK AND A LESBIAN BAR.

BARNETT SLEPIAN

DR. BARNETT SLEPIAN
APRIL 23, 1946 —
OCTOBER 23, 1998

A DOCTOR WHO PROVIDED ABORTIONS, WAS SUBJECTED TO YEARS OF THREATS AND HARASSMENT. MARRIED AND A FATHER OF FOUR. AFTER ATTENDING SYNAGOGUE, HE WAS SHOT THROUGH HIS KITCHEN WINDOW AT HOME IN AMHERST, NEW YORK.

GEORGE TILLER

DR. GEORGE TILLER
AUGUST 8, 1941 —
MAY 31, 2009

A DOCTOR WHO PROVIDED ABORTIONS AND WAS INVOLVED IN REPRODUCTIVE RIGHTS ACTIVISM. FREQUENTLY THREATENED, AND SURVIVED ONE ASSASSINATION ATTEMPT. HE WAS SHOT WHILE AT CHURCH, SERVING AS AN USHER DURING THE SUNDAY MORNING SERVICE, IN WICHITA, KANSAS.

GARRETT SWASEY

GARRETT SWASEY
NOVEMBER 16, 1971 —
NOVEMBER 27, 2015

AN AWARD-WINNING COMPETITIVE ICE SKATER, A FIGURE SKATING COACH, AND A POLICE OFFICER. HE WAS A CO-PASTOR AND ELDER IN HIS CHURCH, MARRIED WITH TWO CHILDREN. SHOT WHILE RESPONDING TO GUNFIRE AT A PLANNED PARENTHOOD OFFICE IN COLORADO SPRINGS, COLORADO.

JENNIFER YURIE AH KING MARKOVSKY

JENNIFER YURIE AH KING MARKOVSKY
DECEMBER 22, 1979 -
NOVEMBER 27, 2015

ORIGINALLY FROM HAWAII, MARRIED WITH TWO CHILDREN. SHE LOVED COOKING AND THE OUTDOORS. SHE WAS ACCOMPANYING A FRIEND TO THE PLANNED PARENTHOOD CLINIC, HER FRIEND WAS ALSO WOUNDED. SHE WAS SHOT IN COLORADO SPRINGS, COLORADO.

KE'ARRE M. STEWART

KE'ARRE M. STEWART
FEBRUARY 9, 1986 —
NOVEMBER 28TH, 2015

AN ARMY VETERAN, AND INSURANCE WORKER, HE WAS MARRIED WITH TWO CHILDREN. HE WAS OUTSIDE THE PLANNED PARENTHOOD CLINIC MAKING A PHONE CALL WHEN HE WAS SHOT. DESPITE HIS INJURY, HE RAN INSIDE THE BUILDING TO WARN PEOPLE, AND CALLED 911. HE WAS SHOT IN COLORADO SPRINGS, COLORADO.

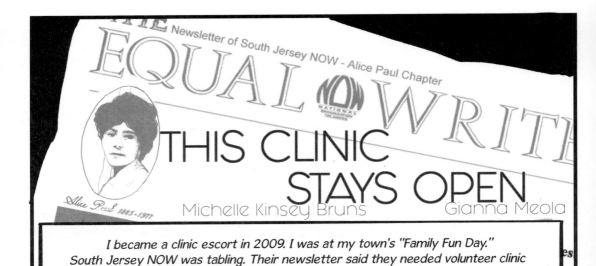

Newsletter of South Jersey NOW - Alice Paul Chapter

THIS CLINIC STAYS OPEN

Michelle Kinsey Bruns   Gianna Meola

I became a clinic escort in 2009. I was at my town's "Family Fun Day." South Jersey NOW was tabling. Their newsletter said they needed volunteer clinic escorts.

It had been 1 week since Dr. George Tiller was shot dead by an anti-choice fanatic.

The day Dr. Tiller died, I was on a fishing boat, returning from working on an ornithological study off the Connecticut shore.

The winds were bad on the sound, and people were holding on for dear life. I sneaked a look at the email on my phone, saw the news, and welled up in tears.

I remembered the anti-abortion terrorism of the '80s, when I was in Catholic school being fed a lot of officious propaganda about the sanctity of life. 1984 had a whole string of bombings. On Christmas Day, all 3 providers in Pensacola, FL, were blown up

"As a birthday gift to Jesus"

I remembered the huge clinic blockades of the late '80s and early '90s, like the ones in Atlanta in 1988, with 1,200 arrests over two months.

And in 1997, I would be horrified to hear that two bombs had gone off at a clinic

5 miles away from where I was sitting at IBM's Atlanta offices where I worked.

I had had an abortion in Atlanta only two years before the bombing there. I'd been 18, recovering from a violent childhood

with a mean drunk of a step-father who beat and kicked and choked me and my mom and my sisters, struggling to build a sane and whole and healthy life on $4.50 an hour.

Neither my recovery from my childhood nor the good career I would later start to build with that job at IBM would have been possible if I'd given birth at 18.

The year after the Atlanta clinic bombing, Eric Robert Rudolph was named as a suspect in not only that bombing, but in bombing an Atlanta lesbian club and the Atlanta Olympics, as well as a fatal Alabama clinic bombing.

It hit literally so close to home.

My city, under attack by Christian terrorism.

But for over a decade beginning in 1998, there would be no more "pro-life" murders. I came to believe the country had gotten past that particular kind of extremism.

When Dr. Tiller was killed in 2009, I was proven wrong. I felt so much: sadness, horror, but more than anything outrage. I had to get involved.

Less than a week after picking up that newsletter, I was in front of the clinic.

My first shift fell on what the escorts called "Circus Day"—a regular clinic harassment field trip by a local Baptist church. Dozens of them, with 6'x12' gore signs, bullhorns, and video cameras, joined the Catholics who showed up daily with handouts full of lies about cancer and infertility and regret. There was also an evangelical biker gang, the most aggressive of all.

Once, one of the bikers trespassed onto our property to approach someone by the entrance. Big dude, boots, bandannas, chains. I got between him and the car. He kept coming until we were chest to chest. The standoff lasted only a minute but felt like forever.

He finally turned and walked back to the sidewalk, where he laughed and smirked at me, posing and pointing at himself, to be sure I knew what a badass he was.

At this clinic, I saw clinic harassers squirt ketchup "blood" on a snowbank, topping it off with a sign about how abortion is murder. I saw them post fake "Closed" signs at the end of our driveway.

I saw them surround a mailman and refuse to let him leave

furious that he had driven around them as they shuffled across the driveway at a snail's pace, moving only enough to technically comply with the federal law against blocking clinic entrances.

Over and over again, I saw them make women cry.

My little clinic in South Jersey was only the start of clinic escorting and clinic defense for me. Days after I started there, anti-choice extremists Operation Rescue announced a press conference at Dr. Tiller's closed clinic in Wichita, KS, not even three weeks after the doctor was killed...

by a man who had the phone number of Operation Rescue's "policy director" (a convicted clinic bomber) on his car's dash when he was arrested.

I was so outraged at the idea of their victory lap, at a doctor's office closed by a murderer they emboldened if not enabled, that I flew to Wichita to help local activists stop Operation Rescue's plan.

We occupied the clinic grounds from dawn 'til nearly dusk. The domestic terrorists did not get their photo op. They had to settle for creeping onto the clinic grounds at sunset, long after any media was gone.

They left some cheap carnations on the lawn and took cell phone pictures for their blog. One of the locals and I came back to pick up every one of the flowers and toss them into the trunk of my rental car. They ended up in a dumpster in Tulsa.

Later that summer, I joined Wichita activists again to assist Omaha, NE, locals in a clinic defense for Dr. Carhart, named by Operation Rescue as the next target of their "activism." They spent 3 days harassing people there, but clinic defenders outnumbered them 2 to 1.

In Louisville, KY, a clinic harasser saw a break appear in the escorts' human chain. He stepped into the gap as I did; I ended up with his crotch pressed into my butt for ten long minutes until he finally gave up.

In Charlotte, NC, defenders on the last day of a week of harassment of clinics, mosques, and progressive Christian churches were so numerous that when the extremists arrived they turned and left, giving one clinic its first protester-free Saturday in eight years.

In Allentown, PA, clinic escorts held up blue plastic tarps to form a privacy tunnel for patients approaching the clinic door, which opened directly onto public property. The bullies would shove pamphlets full of lies under the tarps.

In Jackson, MS, one clinic harasser put his very small child on his shoulders to wave intimidating signs at patients over an eight-foot fence.

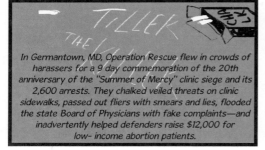

In Germantown, MD, Operation Rescue flew in crowds of harassers for a 9 day commemoration of the 20th anniversary of the "Summer of Mercy" clinic siege and its 2,600 arrests. They chalked veiled threats on clinic sidewalks, passed out fliers with smears and lies, flooded the state Board of Physicians with fake complaints—and inadvertently helped defenders raise $12,000 for low-income abortion patients.

In Montgomery, AL, I saw a guy carrying an American flag with a skull on it, a guy blowing a shofar, and a guy who'd done prison time for burning and bombing clinics in other states.

HELL YEAH! A baby for profit is or you to be FORCED

Replying to @ClinicEscort
@ClinicEscort Oh rly? When was the last incident of "clinic violence"? other than towards the unborn?

@JackYoest
They don't wear BrownSl orange vest emblazoned @bayouchild you got the

I never planned to become a traveling activist or a "thought leader" on clinic harassment and violence. I got involved because I was horrified and furious, and I signed up for a Twitter account (anonymous for the first year and a half) to tell people what happens every day at clinics everywhere.

If a clinic escort different from rolife

Replying to @ClinicEscort
.@ClinicEscort It could happen. After all, abortionists have been known to eat fetuses.

@ClinicEscort Fuck off baby kille #sickFuck
8:46 AM - 15 Aug 2014

As my online platform grew, I used it to spotlight not only current but historical clinic violence and harassment. At a library in 2015, looking up clinic blockades of years past, I found a New York Times photo on microfiche that took my breath away.

It was the doctor who had done my abortion in 1994, photographed during the Atlanta clinic blockades of 1988. My doctor, who had been so kind to me, who paused in his work to ask if I was okay, who reassured me when I said I was scared. In the picture, my doctor was trying to push through a massive crowd of clinic blockaders to get into his building.

On the day the photo was taken, the "Siege of Atlanta" had been going on for two months. Still, he showed up. Still, he did all he could to get his clinic doors open. He knew that women like me needed him.

If those clinic blockades in Atlanta in 1988 had shut down the clinic I would need in 1994, my life might be totally different. I owe a vast and unpayable debt of gratitude to that doctor, to those who helped him keep his doors open, to everyone who has fought to stop zealots from imposing their constrictive one-size-fits-all plan for the lives of women. To have become one of them, to have offered others the same support that they offered me, is a thing I will always be proud of.

At nineteen years old, during my first year in college,

My first time having sex was also the start of my first pregnancy.

yamani hernandez

choices

art by sharon rimann

My friend and I knew how to prevent pregnancy, but neither of us cared to try.

I was a naturalist, open to motherhood

and the Black Nationalist theories I believed in promoted the idea of building the strength and numbers of the Black family.

It took me a while to figure things out, like why I was suddenly so sick.

I went to St. Louis to see my grandparents for their 40th anniversary

and the next day, I saw my grandmother die.

My partner was there to comfort me over her loss, but I couldn't get the image of her out of my head.

When I found out I was pregnant, I wondered.

Was this her spirit returning to me?

In grief, you try to make sense of things like that.

I have no idea if I can keep this pregnancy.

My new job is bringing in some money, but I'd be on my own.

Hey, now. You know I'll support you no matter what, right?

Of course! Dude, look at me. We need to stick together, I mean it.

...Really? You're, uh. Actually the first person to say that.

Thank you. Really. But I think you gonna have you hands full.

By the next week, I had made my decision.

Planned Parenth

Everything looks good. Are you ready?

As I'll ever be, I guess.

SNIFF

Well, I'll let you get changed. Knock when you're done.

This might feel cold for a sec. Deep breath.

You doing okay?

It was a little uncomfortable, but not painful.

After the recovery room, I was instructed not to eat or drink anything, but I was dying for something to drink.

We stopped for an orange juice.

It proved immediately to be a poor idea.

231

I slept a lot after that. It took a while to heal, to rest. I lost a lot of weight in the process.
People complimented me for it, but it felt gross.

you're disappearing!

lookin NICE

you lo
grea

hey, gorgeous!

It felt like another way for people to lay claim to my body and decisions. I didn't want their praise.
I wanted to be a mother.

I wanted to start a family, even if it wouldn't work out just then— but years later, with college finished, I finally had my chance.

Because of my choice, my kids now have parents who center them in their lives.

Finishing college let me start a career that can not only support my family,

but ensures people everywhere will have access to that same choice.

I joined the National Network of Abortion Funds in 2015.

We provide funding, transportation, legal support, and countless other services to people in need, in addition to campaigning for safe, legal abortions.

I know how vital abortion was for me and my family. I trust other people to make that choice for themselves.

Conversations

By Claudia E. Berger

I was the star of Health in high school.

Can anyone name other alternative forms of birth control?

My mom worked in women's healthcare

The pill, patch, ring, IUD, female condom...

I knew more about ectopic pregnancies, STIs, and sexual health at age 12 than I really needed.

Yes...Um. Anyone else?

By the time I went to college my mom was working for the national office of Planned Parenthood

I got a package from home!

It gave me an odd relationship with sex and pregnancy.

Oh, it's just condoms.

won't lose virginity for another year

So when I woke up on my 20th birthday with my period...

Uhg... cramps. Happy birthday to me.

... I had an odd reaction.

I need to call mom!

One of the other topics I grew up hearing about was the statistics of teen pregnancy.

Hey Mom!

Hey chicken! Happy birthday.

Guess what?

Hm?

I did it!

I beat teen pregnancy!

This is the only birthday where I actually "win!"

I can't ever contribute to teen pregnancy.

Haha, very true!

I always assumed you wouldn't.

But I shouldn't have.

I didn't.

I had an abortion when I was 19.

And I know you could've too.

A few years later, I finally talked to her about what it was like; how it felt.

I found out over spring break my sophomore year.

This was before home pregnancy tests, so I had to bring in a urine sample.

I used a Coffee-Mate container that I forgot to rinse out first.

We're going to need another sample...

I was staying at my grandmother's apartment without my family. I felt so isolated. I couldn't even call your dad to tell him because the only phone was out in the open in the living room.

It wasn't until now at 24 that I really became aware of the reality of her situation.

Just how young she was.

How early this was in my parents' relationship. They had only been dating a few months. My dad considers it a turning point in their relationship.

Hey. How are you feeling?

You can't just go back to how things were before. We went through this together.

And how hard it would have been to do this without her family's help and support.

scratch

I cannot imagine going through this without her help.

This made me realize my own prejudice I held against unplanned pregnancy, in particular teen pregnancy. I saw it as something to "beat."

But my mom, my hero, had been pregnant at 19 and it didn't hinder her in any way from accomplishing amazing things with her life.

I really find my 20 year old self particularly cringe worthy. I'm glad how far I've come, but I know I have farther to go.

Why didn't you tell Roberta?*

I was disappointed in my self and I didn't want her to be too.

*my grandmother

Do you think it still affects you?

Oh yes.

I still think about it regularly.

I'd have a 41 year old right now.

I also think about how bad of an experience the clinic was.

Is that why you wanted to work in women's health?

So no one else felt like that?

No. I had already wanted to.

It was my dream to run a Planned Parent-hood clinic since high school.

HOW HAVING AN ABORTION CHANGED A REPRODUCTIVE RIGHTS ACTIVIST

BY MALLORY MCMASTER
ILLUSTRATION BY KATE KERNS

I FIRST NOTICED SOMETHING WAS OFF WHEN MY WEDDING DRESS WOULDN'T ZIP UP.

WHEN I GOOGLED MY SYMPTOMS, THE FIRST THING TO COME UP WAS A PREGNANCY BLOG.

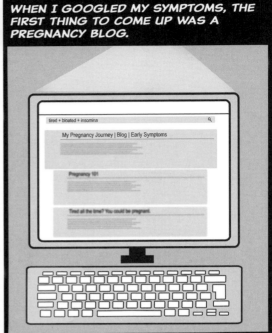

IMMEDIATELY I KNEW I HAD TO HAVE AN ABORTION. I KNEW I DIDN'T WANT TO BE TIED TO MY RELATIONSHIP FOREVER. IT WAS TOXIC. BUT I DIDN'T HAVE THE TOOLS TO GET OUT OF IT. FORTUNATELY, MY HUSBAND SUPPORTED MY CHOICE.

THE CLINIC WAS CLOSED FOR NEW YEARS AND WAITING FOR IT TO REOPEN WAS PAINFUL. I WAS MISERABLE BEING PREGNANT. I DIDN'T FEEL LIKE MYSELF AND I HAD TO WAIT, AND WAIT, AND WAIT.

I WAS NEWLY MARRIED WHEN I FOUND OUT I WAS PREGNANT. BUT I KNEW I DIDN'T WANT TO HAVE KIDS WITH HIM, BE TIED TO HIM FOREVER. THE RELATIONSHIP WAS AWFUL AND ABUSIVE.

THE ABORTION WOULD HELP ME END THE RELATIONSHIP.

I HAD BEEN MARRIED FOR LESS THAN A MONTH

WHEN I FINALLY TALKED TO THE CLINIC IT WAS AN INSTANT RELIEF. I FELT UNDERSTOOD AND SAFE, THEY WALKED ME THROUGH EVERYTHING. MY INSURANCE WOULD COVER THE ABORTION AND I HAD MY APPOINTMENT.

IT'S GOING TO BE OK. WE'LL SEE YOU AT 3.

THANK YOU!

GOING INTO THE CLINIC WE WERE SCREAMED AT BY PROTESTERS. I HAD A HARD TIME KEEPING MY HUSBAND CALM.

IT LOOKED LIKE THE STAFF WAS HAVING A TOUGH DAY AND I WANTED TO DO SOMETHING KIND FOR THEM.

WE BROUGHT DONUTS.

IT WAS SO QUIET IN THE WAITING ROOM. THE ONE THING I REGRET IS NOT TALKING TO ANYONE, NOT STARTING A CONVERSATION.

THE PROCEDURE
THE DAY OF I WAS FEELING AWFUL, BLOATED AND NAUSEOUS. THE PROCEDURE WAS REALLY QUICK AND I DON'T REMEMBER MUCH. WHEN I WOKE UP I FELT THE NAUSEA SETTLE.
I FELT LIKE MYSELF AGAIN.

BEFORE

AFTER

WE DROVE HOME SOON AFTER. I WAS ABLE TO EAT. I STAYED HOME WITH NETFLIX AND THE NEXT DAY I WENT TO WORK. I FELT HUMAN AGAIN.

NETFLIX

HAVING AN ABORTION CHANGED THE PATH MY LIFE WAS ON. THIS WAS THE FIRST STEP IN INVESTING IN MY FUTURE. IT GAVE ME CONFIDENCE IN MYSELF AND PERSPECTIVE ON MY ABUSIVE MARRIAGE. OVER THE NEXT FOUR YEARS I ENDED THE MARRIAGE, WENT BACK TO SCHOOL, BOUGHT A HOUSE, STARTED A CAREER I LOVE, RE-MARRIED, AND NOW WE'RE STARTING A FAMILY.

4 YEARS LATER

UNIVERSITY

Wanted
Bree Jordan

You know I wanted you, right?

I do know.

I know my mother loved me from the moment she held me.

But I also know it's more complicated than that.

I know she was too young.

I know she was too sick.

I know she loved me

But he

SLAM

didn't.

I know we were hungry

And cold

And I know now that it wasn't normal.

I know what she lost.

Her childhood

tic tic

60

Her education

Everything she thought her life would be

Ding!

It all evaporated with two little lines.

I guess I just. . .

I wish I could give some of it back.

It's worth it

if you want it.

"Underwater" - CB Hart

...then I said to Greg, it's not ⌐~⌐.....~_~⌐.... running all. If it were a ⌐~⌐.......the small rotator, then e obviously. But he says that it's ⌐~⌐.... at all, whic course. But ⌐ ~⌐.....⌐... Not at ⌐... I said, if he can go ⌐... and take a look ⌐... what ha

Want to hop by the pond? I have a half hour to kill.

What's wrong with your place? We never go there, and it's closer.

You don't want to go there. The pond will be great.

Hey, Kath. Are you free? I need to talk.

Hey Lani! Come in!

Tony, you left your toys in the hallway!

Hey Danny, Aunt Lani and I are going to talk. Can you go play in your room?

Do you want something to drink? I have fresh or brine.

Brine's fine.

Here you go.

Thanks.

How's Cecilia?

Good! I just put her to nap. Want to go peek?

She's getting so big now!

I think she looks just like Chris.

She's got your eyes.

It's funny. I never thought I'd be Mrs. Mom.

Chris and I thought we'd stop at one. But, look at us now. I was even showing off anemone pics at the canal station yesterday.

Can I ask you something?

Shoot.

Did you... Did you ever have any, before Chris?

Of course.

Would you like to see them?

Here they are.

Go ahead and take a look.

They won't grow any bigger like this. But all they need is a little sunlight and they're fine on their own.

I keep them as reminders of where I was and where I am. They help me put the past behind me.

Without forgetting it's created who I've become.

You should go see mom and dad. They're only just over the hill.

I'm going to go check on the kids, but say hi to them for me, will you?

Don't forget, they're celebrating their 50th in two weeks! No skipping!

Hi, mom and dad.

Kath says hi.

I know it's been a while. It's just been busy.

Nothing major. My dissertation's going fine, it's just getting everything together, you know how it is.

"TIKKUN OLAM" BY ANISE SIMON AND SARAH CROWE

I GUESS I THOUGHT MY RADICAL UPBRINGING COULD SOMEHOW SHIELD ME FROM ABUSIVE MEN, AS IF VIOLENCE DOESN'T FIND US IN EVERY GENERATION AND WEAVE STRAIGHT PAST OUR SENSES.

EVENTUALLY, I KNEW I WAS A PERSON
WHO COULD NOT STAY WITH HIM.

EPILOGUE

I HAVE BEEN PRO-CHOICE SINCE I WAS A CHILD. AS A TEENAGER, I DEBATED MY PEERS IN FAVOR OF CHOICE AND ATTENDED PRO-CHOICE RALLIES.

NEVERTHELESS, I WAS TOTALLY UNPREPARED FOR THE EMOTIONAL DEVASTATION OF BECOMING PREGNANT AND NEEDING AN ABORTION IN MY JUNIOR YEAR OF COLLEGE. EMOTIONAL TRAUMA FOLLOWING AN ABORTION IS A STIGMATIZED TOPIC, AS FEELINGS OF POST-ABORTION GUILT ARE OFTEN WEAPONIZED BY ANTI-CHOICE GROUPS.

I HAVE READ THAT THE BEST INDICATOR OF YOUR MENTAL STATE FOLLOWING AN ABORTION IS YOUR MENTAL STATE BEFORE THE ABORTION. MY ABORTION CAME AT A VERY DIFFICULT TIME, WHEN I WAS VIOLENTLY DEPRESSED, DEEPLY ANXIOUS, UNSURE OF MY FUTURE, AND TRAPPED IN A TOXIC RELATIONSHIP.

IN MY MENTALLY ILL STATE I PERCEIVED MY ABORTION AS A FAILURE TO SERVE MY PURPOSE, RENDERING ME USELESS AND CUT OFF FROM HUMANITY. I REFUSED TO OPEN UP ABOUT MY FEELINGS WITH ANYONE.

SINCE THEN I'VE MADE MAJOR PROGRESS WITH MY MENTAL HEALTH, AND I HAVE BEEN WORKING ON PROCESSING MY ABORTION COMPASSIONATELY. I WAS HELPED ALONG THE WAY BY SO MANY PEOPLE WHO SHARED THEIR DIVERSE EXPERIENCES WITH ABORTION.

IT WAS EQUALLY IMPORTANT FOR ME TO SEE UNAPOLOGETIC, BOLD, POSITIVE STORIES AS IT WAS FOR ME TO SEE STORIES THAT ACKNOWLEDGED THE SHAME AND SADNESS.

AS MY FRIENDS BEGAN HAVING CHILDREN, I FELT REASSURED THAT MY CHOICE TO ABORT WAS THE RIGHT ONE. I HAVE SEEN NEW MOTHERS SPEAK FREELY ABOUT ABORTIONS THEY HAD BEFORE THEY WERE READY TO RAISE CHILDREN.

I AM IN AWE AT THE STRENGTH AND BRILLIANCE OF THESE NEW PARENTS AND I KNOW NOW MORE THAN EVER THAT IF I BECOME A PARENT, I WANT TO BE PREPARED AND CONFIDENT, NOT TERRIFIED AND FILLED WITH SELF-DOUBT AS I WAS WHEN I WAS 20.

THERE ARE MANY HOTLINES AVAILABLE FOR PEOPLE WHO WANT TO TALK ABOUT THEIR ABORTIONS IN A NON-JUDGMENTAL ENVIRONMENT. I WISH I HAD TAKEN ADVANTAGE OF THESE OPTIONS WHEN I WAS YOUNGER. I ENCOURAGE ANYONE WHO'S HURTING TO TAKE CARE OF YOURSELF AND SEEK HELP, YOU ABSOLUTELY DESERVE IT.

SOPHIA FOSTER-DIMINO

DAY 1 : NOV 9th, 2016

NOTHING FEELS REAL.

an abortion diary

by Vreni

It hits me when the owner of the pet store begins to cry.

My vision goes blurry. I feel nauseous. But I've felt nauseous all month.

I want to do something. Everyone online says "Donate!"

Which is all well and good, except I've just applied for food stamps.

An IUD sounds like a good idea. But they can't put one in if you're pregnant.

I've told myself the nausea and the weight gain is from stress. And the last two months have been very stressful.

But I haven't gotten my period in over a month. It's happened before, but this feels different.

I have to know. I make an appointment at a clinic that give free pregnancy tests and ultrasounds.

DAY 2: NOV 10th

The clinic had good Google reviews. The waiting room is perfectly sterile.

A pretty smiling young woman tells me to wait for my counselor, another pretty, smiling woman.

She takes me into a room like a therapist's office. It puts me on edge.

She askes me if I'd thought about what I'd do if the test is positive. I can't say "abortion" but I get my point across.

The same mold of woman gives me a cup, a pipette, and a test strip. She says it might take awhile.

It doesn't.

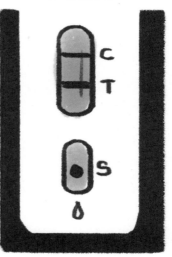

I'm not entirely surprised. But it doesn't feel real.

They keep asking if I want tea. I give in just so they'll stop bothering me about it.

im v pregnant :/

The counselor tells me it's ok if I need time to think about it. I don't want time. I want an ultrasound.

DAY 2: Continued

The ultrasound tech is the only person who isn't smiling. The machine is cold.

She asked if I want to know how far along it is. I do.

14 weeks.

I can't believe it. That's into the second trimester. "I've had my period since then" I explained.

"Well you must have gotten the date wrong," the tech said. "Obviously you did."

In the little room the counselor askes me to consider my options. She tells me her baby was a surprise.

What options? I haven't paid rent in two months. But it's more than money.

I don't want a baby. I don't want to be a mother. Not now.

But no one there asks me what I want.

DAY 3: NOV 11th

Lying in bed, he asks me what's wrong.

He asks if it's about my stomach aches. I nod.

I hadn't wanted to worry him. He's the only one working, for a shady company that won't give him benefits.

He'd had his suspicions when I didn't have my period.

I snap at him. "Why are you tracking my period?!"

I snap at him. "Why are you tracking my period?!"

He's taken aback. "Because I want to be involved in your life."

I've learned to distrust men, to question their motives and be vigilant always.

He makes me feel crazy for thinking that.

I don't know how I could do this without him.

I'm too far along to take the abortion pill, which is safe up to 10 weeks.

From 10 to 16 weeks vacuum aspiration is used. It's a surgical procedure and I'm terrified.

I'm also worried about the cost. I don't want to empty our savings account over this.

By the third clinic I call I can say "I'm calling about an abortion" without stumbling.

One clinic is $420 "plus labwork" (she can't tell me how much labwork is), another is $650 "for everything", another was $720.

I google "how to pay for an abortion" and find helpful information on the National Network of Abortion Funds site.

I end up calling Planned Parenthood and when I explain my situation they set me up with a financial counselor.

I tell the counselor how much I make ($0 currently) how much my boyfriend makes, and our rent.

She says I qualify for emergency Medicaid and the whole procedure will be covered. I'm so relieved I cry.

DAY5: NOV 13th

The abortion is scheduled. It's actually happening. I thought I'd feel relieved.

I've been throwing up for months, have heartburn constantly, and my breasts are huge and super sensitive.

I don't feel relieved. I feel weirdly guilty.

It's hard not to think about the fetus as a baby. As my baby.

Back when I had a salary I had the "baby madness." For two months I couldn't stop thinking about babies.

But the thoughts never felt like mine. It was like someone was inside my head, telling my how great life would be with a baby.

This felt the same way. These thoughts were outside my logical mind, but that didn't stop them.

Maybe it's some internalized version of every hallmark abortion story: the poor, tragic mother, the baby she wants but can't have.

Or maybe I'm just scared that if I do this now the door to motherhood will be closed forever. I don't know if I want that.

DAY 6: NOV 14th

I've told my best friend, and my boyfriend, but I haven't told my mother.

My mom told me and my sisters not to have kids before we're 30, and she always had NARAL and NOW bumper stickers.

I know she'd be supportive of me, but I feel stupid. I'd been on the pill and I fucked up.

When I call her I make small talk for an hour before I can work up the nerve.

She's suprised more than anything else. She knew I'd been sick but had never considered this.

Then she told me when she first moved in with my dad, before they were married, she'd had one too.

I'd had no idea. But suddenly all the anxiety about the abortion was gone.

This wasn't going to ruin me. This was going to make things better when and if I want a baby.

I was ready for the next day. And all the days after.

DAY 7: NOV 15th

My best friend and my boyfriend come with me. I leave them in the waiting room, past the metal detectors.

I wasn't allowed to eat or drink after midnight but I don't feel nauseous. I don't feel anything.

There's one last counseling session. She asks if I want birth control. I've decided on Mirena, an IUD that lasts 5 years.

She asks if I want to see the ultrasounds they took. I say yes this time. I'm curious.

The first picture is a lump. She tells me the lump is fourteen weeks and three days old.

The second is a human skull. A tiny human skull, growing inside my body.

I put on a very awkward robe and some slippers. I try to keep myself covered as a nurse explains the next step.

They'll give my some pills to help soften my cervix so the fetus can be removed without tearing anything.

They sit me in a nice recliner with the pills in my lip. I have to wait 90 minutes for them to dissolve.

287

DAY 7: Continued

Dazed women hobble back to the recovery area, robes open, leaking blood.

I try to read a magazine but the words are fuzzy. I wish there was a tv. I feel so cold.

A nurse sees me shivering and tucks a blanket around me, just like my mom used to.

They call my name. The operating room is small. The doctors are kind and calm.

I start crying as the anesthesiologist puts a needle in my hand. I'm thinking about the skull.

They look concerned. "I'm ok," I tell them, "I just hate needles."

I'm still crying when I wake up in the chair. My insides are screaming.

The nurse from before holds my hand and tells me about her plans for Thanksgiving. By the time she's done describing the feast, the pain is gone.

My closest friends are waiting for me outside. I feel free, almost euphoric. I can't wait to eat my weight in rice balls and bubble tea.

They said it can take 6 weeks to 6 months for your body return to a pre pregnancy state. And I'm also adjusting to the IUD.

I'm learning my menstural cycle all over again. I spot and cramp a lot, but my moods are much more stable than on the pill.

Only one of my breasts got smaller. It's like half of my body still thinks I'm pregnant.

The cloud of depression that lingered for three months is gone.

I still feel angry, and lost, and frightened, but after I cry I can get up and get on with my life.

I've told some of my friends, but not all of them. It's a hard thing to just bring up in conversation.

But I wish I'd had a friend who I could talk to about what was happening to me.

I wanted so badly for someone to tell me my mixed emotions were normal, my fears were normal, my whole situation was normal.

We need to be reminded how normal abortion is, now more than ever. And now I can be that friend.

Lizartistry
lizartistry.com

Lizartistry, she/they, creates digital art, most often in the form of visual notes, guided by a passion for lifelong learning and revolutionary praxis.

Leah Nichols
mrawmraw.squarespace.com

Leah Nichols is a San Francisco/Seoul-based designer seeking to expand models of kinship, increase access to collective histories, and champion the compatibility of joy and trauma.

Ke'Asia Brown
janesdueprocess.org

Since navigating the legal system as a teen seeking abortion care, Ke'Asia Brown has become passionate about fighting for the reproductive rights of all young people in Texas.

Alicia

Alicia is a Jane's Due Process Youth Advocacy Fellow and former client. She had her first child at 15 and when she found out she was pregnant again at 16, she sought the help of Jane's Due Process for judicial bypass support.

Maddie Dennis
maddiedennis.com

Maddie Dennis is an animator and comic artist who loves worms. She lives in Providence, RI, and teaches both comics and animation up in Boston. Her dream is to become covered in thick moss.

Hazel Newlevant
newlevant.com

Hazel is a cartoonist and editor whose comics include *No Ivy League*, *Sugar Town*, and *If This Be Sin*. They live with their cats in Brooklyn.

MJ Flores

MJ Flores is a storyteller with We Testify, a program of the National Network of Abortion Funds, and shares her story to confront abortion stigma and challenge anti-abortion legislation.

Kat Fajardo
katfajardo.com

Kat Fajardo (they/she) is a Honduran Colombian award-winning cartoonist and illustrator. They are the creator of *Miss Quinces*, which was a National Indie Bestseller and received two starred reviews.

Kendra Josie Kirkpatrick
kendrajosiekirkpatrick.com

Kendra Josie Kirkpatrick enjoys large amounts of black on both her comic pages and her clothes, and has a passion for music that features people screaming. BFA Cartooning, SVA '16.

Jennifer Camper
jennifercamper.com

Jennifer Camper's books include *Rude Girls and Dangerous Women* and *subGURLZ*, and she edits the anthology *Juicy Mother*. She is the founding director of the Queers & Comics Conference.

Dr. Cynthia Greenlee
twitter.com/CynthiaGreenlee

Dr. Cynthia Greenlee is a North Carolina-based journalist and historian. She's the senior editor at *Rewire*, the go-to website about reproductive justice, health, and rights in the United States.

Jaz Malone
jazimated.com

Jaz Malone lives in Philadelphia, PA, where she currently studies UX design and works as a sequential artist, an arts instructor, and a death doula.

Rickie Solinger

Rickie Solinger is a curator and a historian. She is the author or editor of eleven books about reproductive politics and satellite issues.

Rachel Merrill

rachelmerrill.net

Rachel Merrill was born and raised in Baton Rouge, Louisiana and now lives in the much colder Astoria, Queens. She enjoys beer and donuts, but not together.

Rachel Wilson

rachelwilson.contently.com

Rachel Wilson is a writer from the UK whose work has appearead on *i-D*, *The Guardian*, *Broadly*, *Noisey*, and more. She also grapples with her hand-me-down film camera sometimes.

Ally Shwed

allyshwed.com

Ally Shwed is a cartoonist who specializes in comics journalism and nonfiction. Her work has been published by First Second Books, *The Nib*, *Vox*, and *The Boston Globe*.

Hallie Jay Pope

graphicadvocacy.org

Hallie Jay Pope is a lawyer/cartoonist living in Washington, DC. She runs the Graphic Advocacy Project, a nonprofit that uses visual communication tools to explain legal concepts.

Anna Sellheim

annasellheim.com

Anna Sellheim graduated from the Center For Cartoon Studies in 2016. She has had her work featured on *The Nib*, *Upworthy*, and a bunch of cool anthologies. She moves around a lot.

Brittany Mostiller

Brittany Mostiller is the executive director of the Chicago Abortion Fund, a nonprofit that promotes reproductive justice through funding abortion and organizing for racial, economic, and gender justice.

Lilly Taing
lillytaingart.wixsite.com/portfolio

Lilly Taing is a Chinese-Cambodian American artist who loves reading and telling stories. She likes playing with colors and shapes and trying to capture quiet, mundane moments in life in extraordinary ways.

Lindsay Rodriguez
abortionfunds.org

Lindsay Rodriguez is the Communications Manager for the National Network of Abortion Funds. She joined NNAF after serving as Board President for the Lilith Fund for Reproductive Equity.

Lucy Haslam
lucyhaslam.com

Lucy Haslam graduated from Falmouth University, UK and now specialises in editorial work and comics. Some of these comics are made as part of the group Froglump.

Samantha Romero

Samantha Romero was an organizer for the Wendy Davis Campaign, which sparked her passion for reproductive justice. She is the President of the West Fund, and a member of We Testify.

Erin Lux
erin-lux.com

Erin Lux is a Brooklyn-based illustrator and cartoonist. She's the creator of the webcomic _Fascist Friends_, and many other short irreverent comics.

Candice Russell

Candice Russell is a writer and abortion storyteller whose work has been featured in *Teen Vogue*, *ELLE*, *Glamour*, and *The Huffington Post*. She serves on the board of NARAL Pro-Choice Texas.

Laura Lannes

lauralannes.com

Laura Lannes is a cartoonist and illustrator from Brazil living in New York City. She is the editor of the *Bad Boyfriends* anthology.

Heidi Williamson

Heidi Williamson is the Senior Policy Analyst for the Women's Health and Rights program at the Center for American Progress and the Center for American Progress Action Fund. She is an avid comic book reader.

Cielo Krase

wasteofpaint.net

Cielo Krase is a trans male who lives quietly with his partner and two cats, Pickle Chip and Honey. When not working at his day job he can be found at home working on art projects or indulging in internet culture.

Cathy Camper

cathycamper.com

Cathy Camper is the author of the award-winning *Lowriders in Space* graphic novel series, *Ten Ways to Hear Snow*, *Bugs Before Time*, and *Arab Arab All Year Round*. Cathy is a librarian and lives in Portland, Oregon.

Kriota Willberg

kriotawelt.blogspot.com

Kriota Willberg is the inaugural Artist-In-Residence at the New York Academy of Medicine. She is best known for her comics about injury prevention for cartoonists and artists.

Dr. Katherine Brown

Dr. Katherine Brown is an Assistant Professor in the Department of Obstetrics, Gynecology, and Reproductive Sciences at the University of California, San Francisco. She provides full-spectrum reproductive healthcare, including abortion care!

Andrew Carl

andrewcarlcomics.com

Andrew Carl is an Eisner and Harvey Award-winning editor and writer for comics. His upcoming series, *Only Hope*, explores things deeply important to his psyche: anxiety, depression, and talking cats.

Seth Smith

sethssmithart.com

Seth Smith is an award-winning comic artist based on the east coast. His passion for comics comes from his background in communications and a formal artistic education in illustration and a degree in comics from SCAD Atlanta.

Benita Ulisano

clinicvestproject.org

Benita Ulisano is a longtime abortion rights activist, clinic escort and founder of The Clinic Vest Project.

Laura Martin

theartof-larel.tumblr.com

Laura Martin is a graduate of the Center for Cartoon Studies in White River Junction, VT. When she's not drawing comics, she likes reading, playing video games, and jumping into very deep, cold bodies of water.

Steph Kraft Sheley

Stephanie Kraft Sheley, JD, MHA is the founder and project director of Right By You, a text line that helps Missourians access abortion care. She is the principal attorney of Kraft Sheley Law, LLC, a law practice focused on abortion and birth, serves on the board of the Birth Rights Bar Association, and is a full-spectrum doula and childbirth educator.

Plan C

plancpills.org

Plan C is a public health meets creative campaign to transform access to abortion in the U.S. by normalizing the self-directed option of abortion pills by mail.

Nomi Kane

nomikane.com

Nomi Kane is an alumnus of The Center for Cartoon Studies who draws editorial cartoons and short fiction comics whenever she can. By day, she works as a Staff Artist at the Schulz Studio.

Sarah Mirk

mirkwork.com

Sarah "Shay" Mirk (she/they) is a graphic jour- nalist, editor, and teacher. She is the author of *Guantanamo Voices*, an illustrated oral history of Guantanamo Bay prison.

Kris Louis Weaver

linkedin.com/in/kris-weaver-374b2496

Kris Louis Weaver is an illustrator, cartoonist, graphic designer, and character designer originally from Long Island, New York. They have a cat named Charlie and they love fun facts and dad jokes.

Eliot Lady

Eliot Lady lives in queens with a thousand hungry ghosts and a cat. They "quit" art and now hoard their comics all for themself while working as a mental health provider.

Sage Coffey

sagecoffey.com

Sage Coffey is a nervous little cartoonist gremlin. They like to make comics that make them laugh and then cry and if they're lucky, laugh again.

Rachel Hays

Rachel Hays is a writer and the owner/operator of risograph micropress Taxonomy Press. She lives in Detroit with her white pitbull Audrey, who graciously posed for this comic back in 2016.

Leah Hayes
leahhayes.com

Leah Hayes is an illustrator, musician, song-writer, and producer. She is the creator of the graphic novel *Not Funny Ha-Ha*. She works out of New York City and Los Angeles.

Tanya DePass
ineeddiversegames.org

Tanya DePass is the founder and Director of I Need Diverse Games, a not-for-profit foundation based in Chicago dedicated to better diversification of all aspects of gaming.

Wren Chavers
wren.best

Wren Chavers a recent graduate of the School of Visual Arts, and they're working to make all the comics they can! When they aren't making comics, they're making memes or bread.

Tatiana Gill
tatianagill.com

Tatiana Gill is a Seattle-based cartoonist whose art includes themes of body-positivity, feminism, mental health and recovery. She has created dozens of self-published comics.

Mick Moran
meetmickmoran.com

Mick Moran is a radical full-spectrum doula and the editor of The Doula Project's zine, *DIY Doula: Self-Care for Before, During, & After Your Abortion.*

Archie Bongiovanni
archiebongiovanni.com

Archie Bongiovanni is a cartoonist and illustrator living in Minneapolis. Their graphic novel, *A Quick And Easy Guide To They/Them Pronouns* was published with Limerence Press/Oni Press.

Daniela Diaz

Daniela Diaz is a We Testify abortion storyteller. Her advocacy and activism focuses strongly on the intersection of reproductive justice, HIV/AIDS and immigration from a global perspective.

Stephanie Rodriguez
stephguez.com

Stephanie Rodriguez is a Bronx-born comic book artist and illustrator. She graduated from the School of Visual Arts in 2011. Stephanie creates illustrations and self-published comics depicting the highs and lows of everyday life.

Renee Bracey Sherman
reneebraceysherman.com

Renee Bracey Sherman is the founder and executive director of We Testify, an organization dedicated to the leadership and representation of people who have abortions.

Kennedy Tarrell
kennedraw.tumblr.com

Kennedy Tarrell is a Storyboard Revisionist at DreamWorks Animation Television on *Spirit Riding Free*. They draw horses during the day and comics at night.

Katie Fricas
klongua.com

Katie Fricas is a cartoonist and illustrator in New York City. She has published political comics in *The Guardian* and is the creator of the pop culture zine *Fashionique*.

Michelle Kinsey Bruns
michellekinseybruns.com

Michelle Kinsey Bruns is an advocate for safety and privacy of abortion clinic patients and staff, and has been a clinic escort or clinic defender at anti-choice protests in nine states.

Gianna Meola
giannameola.com

Gianna Meola graduated from the School of Visual Arts with a BFA in Illustration. She enjoys traveling, sketching, and going on walks.

Jensine Eckwall
jensineeckwall.com

Jensine Eckwall is a Brooklyn-based illustrator whose work has been honored by the Society of Illustrators, *American Illustration*, *Spectrum Fantastic Art*, and *3x3*.

Yamani Hernandez
abortionfunds.org

Yamani Hernandez is the Executive Director of the National Network of Abortion Funds, which works with member organizations to remove barriers to abortion access.

Sharon Rimann
phlegmmefatale.tumblr.com

Sharon Rimann was born in Missouri in 1993, and started drawing soon after. They are mostly self-taught, but will concede some credit to Bob Ross, Mike Mignola, and the devil.

Claudia E. Berger
claudiaeberger.com

Claudia E. Berger is a NYC-based cartoonist. She makes comics about mental health, mythology, and houseplants, and spends way too much time thinking about science fiction.

Mallory McMaster
twitter.com/malloryinpink

Mallory McMaster is an abortion activist, dog mom, terrible cook, and cleaning enthusiast hailing from Cleveland, OH.

Kate Kerns
katekerns.com

Kate Kerns is a graphic designer and illustrator from Kansas, now living in Austin, TX. She has worked as a victim advocate for the National Domestic Violence Hotline.

Bree Jordan
bree-jordan.weebly.com

Bree Jordan is a Salt Lake City-based comic artist and health care professional. Her work is frequently concerned with bodily autonomy, patient advocacy, and end of life planning.

CB Hart

instagram.com/explodinglobstercomics
CB Hart is a cartoonist living in San Mateo and graduate of the Sequential Artist Workshop.

Anise Simon

Anise Simon works as the Southern Funds Coordinator at the National Network of Abortion Funds, where she provides support to grassroots abortion funds in the South.

Sarah Crowe

eworcharas.com
Sarah Crowe is a sculptor and cartoonist made in Austin, but made for New York.

Sophia Foster-Dimino

hellophia.com
Sophia Foster-Dimino is a cartoonist and illustrator.

Vreni

stillvreni.com
Vreni received her BFA in Cartooning from the School of Visual Arts. She loves making comics that inform and inspire. When not drawing she's falling down YouTube rabbit holes, playing puzzle games, and taking long naps. She lives in New York with her husband and cat.

Pam Wishbow

pamwishbow.com
Pam Wishbow went to school for illustration, and bounced a few times on her way from her childhood home in NJ to her new home in Seattle. She lives with her cats, Earthling and Guy.

Selected Bibliography

Undue Burdens
by Hallie Jay Pope

Access Denied: Origins of the Hyde Amendment and Other Restrictions on Public Funding for Abortion. Retrieved from https://www.aclu.org/other/access-denied-origins-hyde-amend-ment-and-other-restrictions-public-funding-abor-tion

Arons, J. (2013, May 10). How the Hyde Amendment Discriminates Against Poor Women and Women of Color. Retrieved from https://www.americanprogress.org/issues/women/news/2013/05/10/62875/how-the-hyde-amend-ment-discriminates-against-poor-women-and-women-of-color/

—. (2016, September 23). Opinion: The Hyde Amendment Hurts Poor Women of Color the Most. *Newsweek*. Retrieved from http://www.news-week.com/hyde-amendment-hurts-poor-women-color-most-501763

Fact Sheet: The Hyde Amendment. Retrieved from http://allaboveall.org/wp/wp-content/uploads/2015/06/Hyde-Amendment-Fact-Sheet-011717.pdf

Talbot, M. (2017, January 25). Daily Comment: Trump Makes the Global Gag Rule on Abortion Even Worse. *The New Yorker*. Retrieved from http://www.newyorker.com/news/daily-comment/trump-makes-the-global-gag-rule-on-abortion-even-worse

Urban Institute analysis of DYNASIM for the Kaiser Family Foundation. (2013, July 15). Median Income Among Medicare Beneficiaries, Overall and by Race/Ethnicity, Age, and Gender, 2012. Retrieved from http://kff.org/medicare/slide/me-dian-income-among-medicare-beneficiaries-over-all-and-by-raceethnicity-age-gender-2012/

Horror Stories
by Jennifer Camper

Blanchard, K., et al. (2010, November 24). Self-induction of abortion among women in the United States. *Reproductive Health Matters*, 18(36), 136-146.

No Child Left Behind. (2017, February). *Harper's Magazine*,

Abortion Trials
written by Rickie Solinger
art by Rachel Merrill

Solinger, R. (1994). *The Abortionist: A Woman Against the Law*. New York, NY: The Free Press,

Jane
written by Rachel Wilson
art by Ally Shwed

Bart, P. B. (1987). Seizing the Means of Re-production: An Illegal Feminist Abortion Col-lective—How and Why it Worked. *Qualitative Sociology*, 10(4). Retrieved from https://auto-maticwriting1.files.wordpress.com/2013/07/seiz-ing-the-means-of-reproduction.pdf

Kaplan, L. (1995). *The Story of Jane: The Legendary Underground Feminist Abortion Service*. Chicago, IL: UChicago Press,

Ross, L. J. (1998). African-American Wom-en and Abortion. In R. Solinger (Ed.), *Abortion Wars: A Half-Century of Struggle* (pp.161-207), Berkeley and Los Angeles, CA: University of California Press. Retrieved from http://www.trustblackwomen.org/2011-05-10-03-28-12/publi-cations-a-articles/african-americans-and-abor-tion-articles/31-african-american-wom-en-and-abortion

Body & Soul, Science & Religion:
All Crowded Into One Uterus
by Kriota Willberg

Baday, A. B. Khitamy. (2013). Divergent Views on Abortion and The Period of Ensoulment. *Sultan Qaboos University Medical Journal*, 13(1), 26-31.

Brind'Amour, K. (2007, October 30). Quickening. Retrieved from https://embryo.asu.edu/pages/quickening

Buklijas, T., Hopwood, T. Unborn 1300-1800s. Retrieved from http://www.sites.hps.cam.ac.uk/visibleembryos/s1_3.html

Gatrad, R., et al. (2005). Sikh Birth Customs. *Archives of Disease in Childhood*, 90(6), 560-563.

Hill, M. A. (2017, July 25). Embryology. Retrieved from https://embryology.med.unsw.edu.au/embryology/index.php/Main_Page

Himma, K. E. (2005). A dualist analysis of abortion: personhood and the concept of self qua experiential subject. *Journal of Medical Ethics*, *31*(1), 48-55.

Mayo Clinic. (2017, July 8). Healthy Lifestyle/ Pregnancy Week By Week. Retrieved from http://www.mayoclinic.org/healthy-lifestyle/pregnancy-week-by-week/in-depth/fetal-development/art-20046151?pg=2

Office on Women's Health. (2010, September 27). Stages of pregnancy. Retrieved from https://www.womenshealth.gov/pregnancy/you-are-pregnant/stages-of-pregnancy.html

Rothstein, P. Lung Development. PDF. Prod. Columbia University.

The Baby Center. (2015, August). Fetal Development Week by Week. Retrieved from http://www.babycenter.com/fetal-development-week-by-week

Tsimis, M. E., et al. (2015). Prematurity: present and future. *Mierva Ginecologica*, 67(1), 35-46.

Wikipedia. Ensoulment. Retrieved January 28, 2017 from URL https://en.wikipedia.org/wiki/Ensoulment

Born and Forgotten
written by Dr. Katherine Brown & Andrew Carl, art by Seth Smith

Biggs, M. A., Upadhyay, U. D., McCulloch, C. E., et al. (2017, February). Women's Mental Health and Wellbeing 5 Years After Receiving or Being Denied an Abortion: A Prospective, Longitudinal Cohort Study. *JAMA Psychiatry*, 74(2), 169-178. doi: 10.1001/jamapsychiatry.2016.3478

Committee on Gynecologic Practice. (2009, June). ACOG Committee Opinion No. 434: induced abortion and breast cancer risk. *Obstetrics & Gynecology*, 113(6), 1417-8. doi: 10.1097/AOG.0b013e3181ac067d

Guttmacher Institute. http://guttmacher.org

Lee, S.J., Ralston, H.J., Drey, E.A., Partridge, J.C., Rosen, M.A. (2005, August). Fetal pain: a systematic multidisciplinary review of the evidence. JAMA, 294(8), 947-54. doi: 10.1001/jama.294.8.947

National Center for Environmental Health, Division of Emergency and Environmental Health Services. (2016, September). Childhood Lead Poisoning Data, Statistics, and Surveillance. Retrieved from http://www.cdc.gov/nceh/Lead/data/index.htm

Texas Department of State Health Services. (2016, December). A Woman's Right to Know. Retrieved from http://dshs.texas.gov/wrtk/

—. (2016, September). A Woman's Right to Know Resource Directory. Retrieved from http://dshs.texas.gov/wrtk/

They Can't Get That From Us
by Steph Kraft Sheley

Alazri, M., Heywood, P., Neal, R.D., et al. (2007). How important is continuity of care? *Sultan Oaboos Univ Med J.*, 7(3), 197-206.

Biggs, M.A., Upadhyay, U.D., McCulloch, C.E. et al. (2016). Women's Mental Health and Well-being 5 Years After Receiving or Being Denied an Abortion: A Prospective, Longitudinal Cohort Study. *JAMA Psychiatry*, 74(2), 169-178.

Boodman, S.G. (2009, September 1). Abortion stigma affects doctors' training and choices. *Washington Post*. Retrieved from http://www.washingtonpost.com/wp-dyn/content/article/2009/08/28/AR2009082802785.html

Center for Reproductive Rights & Ibis Reproductive Health. (2014). Evaluating priorities: measuring women's and children's health and well-being against abortion restrictions in the states. Retrieved from https://www.ibisreproductivehealth.org/sites/default/files/files/publications/Ibis%20and%20CRR_Priorities_Project_FINAL_2014.pdf

Dunn, L. (2011, July 29). 5 tips to improve a hospital's brand. *Becker Hospital Review*. Retrieved from http://www.beckershospitalreview.com/hospital-management-administration/5-tips-to-improve-a-hospitals-brand.html

Flanagan, N. (2016, January). Reputation is everything: how 2 hospitals are weathering PR firestorms. *Healthcare Dive*. Retrieved from http://www.healthcaredive.com/news/reputation-is-everything-how-2-hospitals-are-weathering-pr-firestorms/412982/

Gulliford, M., Nathani, S. & Morgan, M. (2006). What is "continuity of care"? *J. Health Serv. Res. Policy, 11*(4), 248-250.

Induced Abortion in the United States. (2017, January). Retrieved from https://www.guttmacher.org/fact-sheet/induced-abortion-united-states

Jerman, J., Jones, R. K. & Onda, T. (2016, May). Characteristics of U.S. abortion patients in 2014 and changes since 2008. Guttmacher. Retrieved from https://www.guttmacher.org/report/characteristics-us-abortion-patients-2014

Jones, R. K., Jerman, J. (2017). Abortion incidence and service availability in the United States, 2014. *Perspectives on Sexual and Reproductive Health, 49*(1), 17-27.

Kaye, J., Amiri, B., Melling, L. (2016, May). Health care denied: patients and physicians speak out about Catholic hospitals and the threat to women's health and lives. ACLU. Retrieved from https://www.aclu.org/sites/default/files/field_document/healthcaredenied.pdf

Logsdon, M. B., Handler, A., Godfrey, E. M. (2012). Women's preferences for the location of abortion services: a pilot study in two Chicago clinics. *Mat. Child Health J., 16*(1), 212-216.

Martin, L. A., Debbink, M., Hassinger, J., (2014). Measuring stigma among abortion providers: assessing the abortion provider stigma survey instrument. *Women Health, 54*(7), 641-661.

Memo on private insurance coverage of abortion. (2011, January 19). Guttmacher. Retrieved from https://www.guttmacher.org/article/2011/01/memo-private-insurance-coverage-abortion

"No Margin, No Mission" is too simplistic. (2013). *AMA J. Ethics, 15*(2), 101-103.

Norris, A., Bessett, D., Steinberg, J. R., et al (2011). Abortion stigma: a reconceptualization of constitutents, causes and consequences. *Womens Health Issues, 21*(3 Supp), S49-54.

Raymond, E. G., Grimes, D. A., (2012). The comparative safety of legal induced abortion and childbirth in the United States. *Obstet Gynecol, 119*(2 Pt 1), 215-219.

Rodak, S. (2012, July 26). 8 best practices for managing a hospital's reputation. *Beckers Hospital Review*. Retrieved from http://www.beckershospitalreview.com/hospital-management-administration/8-best-practices-for-managing-a-hospitals-reputation.html

Schoen, J. (2013). Living through some giant changes: the establishment of abortion services. *Am. J. Public Health, 103*(3), pp. 416-20.

Sudhakar-Krishan, V., Rudolf, M. C. J. (2007). *Arch Dis Child, 92*(2), 381-383.

United States Conference of Catholic Bishops (2009). Ethical and religious directives for Catholic health care services, fifth edition. Retrieved from http://www.usccb.org/issues-and-action/human-life-and-dignity/health-care/upload/Ethical-Religious-Directives-Catholic-Health-Care-Services-fifth-edition-2009.pdf

University of Chicago. Accessing abortion in Illinois: a guide for health and social service providers: understanding abortion stigma and shame. https://abguide.uchicago.edu/page/understanding-abortion-stigma-and-shame

Upadhyay, U. D., Weitz, T. A., Jones, R. K. (2014). Denial of abortion because of provider gestational age limits in the United States. *Am. J. Public Health, 104*(9), 1687-1694. doi: 10.2105/AJPH.2013.301378

U.S. abortion rate continues to decline, hits historic low. (2017, January 17). Guttmacher. Retrieved from https://www.guttmacher.org/news-release/2017/us-abortion-rate-continues-decline-hits-historic-low

Uttley, L., Reynerston, S., Kenny, L. (2013, December). Miscarriage of medicine: the growth of Catholic hospitals and the threat to reproductive health care. Retrieved from http://static1.1.sqspcdn.com/static/f/816571/24079922/1387381601667/Growth-of-Catholic-Hospitals-2013.pdf?token=pS-DxeBBlXrRZQx%2BPE%2FJwWUkTuD4%3D

Uttley, L., Reynerston, S., Pawelko, R. (n.d.). Merging Catholic and non-sectarian hospitals: NYS Models for addressing ethical challenges. Retrieved from http://static1.1.sqspcdn.com/static/f/816571/23042588/1372882137057/Models+of+Catholic-secular+hospitals+mergers+in+NYS.pdf?token=pSDxeBBlXrRZQx%2BPE%2F2FJwWUkTuD4%3D

Weitz, T. A., Taylor, D., Desai, S., et al. (2013). Safety of aspiration abortion performed by nurse practitioners, certified nurse midwives, and physician assistants under a California legal waiver. *Am. J. Public Health, 103*(3), 454-461.

Plan C
written by Nomi Kane & the Plan
C Team, art by Nomi Kane

Chen, M. J., Creinin, M. D. Mifepristone with buccal misoprostol for medical abortion: a systematic review. *Obstet Gynecol, 2015*(126). 12-21.

Faúndes, A., et al. (2007). Misoprostol for the termination of pregnancy up to 12 completed weeks of pregnancy. *International Journal of Gynecology & Obstetrics, 99*(Supplement 2). S172-S177.

Finer, L. B., Zolna, M. R. (2006). Declines in unintended pregnancy in the United States, 2008-2011. *New England Journal of Medicine, 374*(9), 843-852.

Grossman, D., et al. (2015, November 17). Knowledge, opinion and experience related to abortion self-induction in Texas. Texas Policy Evaluation Project. Retrieved from https://utexas.app.box.com/v/KOESelfInductionResearchBrief

Office of Population Research at Princeton University & Association of Reproductive Health Professionals (2017, January 24). History of Plan B OTC. Retrieved from http://ec.princeton.edu/pills/planbhistory.html

The Right to Remain Unpregnant
by Sarah Mirk

Mirk, S. (2010, February 18). Let's Talk about Sex: Planned Parenthood's President Talks About the New Center. *The Portland Mercury.* Retrieved from http://www.portlandmercury.com/portland/lets-talk-about-sex/Content?oid=2178071

—. (2016, October 31). The Political Power of Telling Abortion Stories. *Bitch Media.* Retrieved from https://bitchmedia.org/article/how-we-talk-about-abortion-election

Popovich, N. (2015, May 6). Colorado contraception program was a huge success—but the GOP is scrapping it. *The Guardian.* Retrieved from https://www.theguardian.com/us-news/2015/may/06/colorado-contraception-family-planning-republicans

Ramsey, L. (2016, December 4). Here's how much an IUD costs with Obamacare—and without. *Business Insider.* Retrieved from http://www.businessinsider.com/how-much-iud-procedures-would-cost-without-obamacare-2016-12

Schencker, L. (2016, December 1). After Trump's win, Planned Parenthood of Illinois reports big spike in IUD appointments. *Chicago Tribune.* Retrieved from http://www.chicagotribune.com/business/ct-trump-birth-control-demand-spike-1202-biz-20161201-story.html

Tabernise, S. (2015, July 5). Colorado's Effort Against Teenage Pregnancies Is a Startling Success. *The New York Times.* Retrieved from https://www.nytimes.com/2015/07/06/science/colorados-push-against-teenage-pregnancies-is-a-startling-success.html

Self Care After Your Abortion
by Rachel Hays

Abortion Aftercare. *Our Bodies, Ourselves* (2014, March 27). Retrieved from http://www.ourbodiesourselves.org/health-info/aftercare/

After the Abortion. Every Woman's Health Centre. Retrieved from http://everywomanshealthcentre.ca/after-the-abortion/

Aftercare Instructions. Feminist Women's Health Center. Retrieved from http://www.feministcenter.org/en/abortion-care/after-care-instructions

Caring for Yourself After an Abortion. Planned Parenthood. Retrieved from https://www.plannedparenthood.org/planned-parenthood-michigan/patient/abortion-services/caring-for-yourself-after-an-abortion

Tips to Speed Recovery After Aboriton. Marie Stopes UK. Retrieved from https://mariestopes.org.uk/women/abortion/abortion-aftercare/tips-speed-recovery-after-abortion

ABORTION BASICS: ACCESS, FUNDING, & HEALTH EDUCATION

Abortion Care Network (abortioncarenetwork.org). An organization that ensures abortion access, supports providers, and fights stigma.

Center for Reproductive Rights (reproduciverights.org). A global legal advocacy organization dedicated to protecting reproductive rights, with a specialization in U.S. constitutional and international human rights law.

Guttmacher Institute (guttmacher.org). A research and policy organization with a focus on sexual and reproductive rights.

National Abortion Federation (prochoice.org). An organization with a mission to ensure safe, legal, and accessible abortions.

National Network of Abortion Funds (abortionfunds.org). A reproductive justice oriented organization that works to provide abortion funds to those in need.

Planned Parenthood (plannedparenthood.org). A national healthcare provider, women's health advocate, and resource for sex education and professional development.

Women's Reproductive Rights Assitance Project (wrrap.org). An organization that provides financial assistance for safe legal abortion and emergency contraception.

HISTORY

"African-American Women and Abortion," Loretta J. Ross, Originally printed in *Abortion Wars: A Half-Century of Struggle*, edited by Rickie Solinger. A comprehensive and powerful history by Loretta J. Ross, the groundbreaking reproductive rights advocate and originator of the concept of reproductive justice. Ross makes connections from white America's ownership of the Black body through slavery to the contemporary challenges disproportionately faced by women of color.

"History of Abortion in the U.S.," *Our Bodies Ourselves*. (http://www.ourbodiesourselves.org/health-info/u-s-abortion-history/). This article from *Our Bodies, Ourselves*, revised August 2022, provides a concise yet thorough introductory history of abortion access in the United States, covering legislative landmarks as well as grassroots initiatives. The piece is supplemented by links to primary sources and collected data as well as quotes from abortion seekers' personal experiences.

"Jane: An Abortion Service," CWLU Herstory Project, 2016. (https://www.cwluherstory.org/jane-abortion-service/?rq=jane%20abortion%20service). An introduction and thorough archive of The Abortion Counseling Service of Women's Liberation, a pre-*Roe v. Wade* network of illegal abortion providers better known as "Jane." The archive, hosted by the Chicago Women's Liberation Union Herstory Project, collects narratives of participants, original documents disseminated by Jane, academic research about Jane, and contemprary art created as a celebration of Jane's legacy.

"Women, Midwives, and Nurses: A History of Women Healers," Barbara Ehrenreich & Deidre English, 1973. Before *Nickel and Dimed* and *Mother Jones*, Barbara Ehrenreich and Deirdre English collaborated on this history of the persectution of women healers in the western world. A well-known feminist text advocating for women to know and trust their own bodies in the face of a patriarchal health system, but its completely Eurocentric approach hasn't aged well.

INTERSECTIONALITY

Philadephia Black Women's Health Project (http://www.blackwomenshealthproject.org/aaabortion.htm). The Philadelphia Black Women's Health Project presents a consice collection of facts about abortion, focusing on the demographic of abortion seekers and factors impacting access. Data is largely sourced from the Guttmacher Institute, Planned Parenthood and the National Abortion Federation. Part of a series of BWHP factsheets on health and reproductive justice written for Black women and families.

Healthcare Bill of Rights (healthcarebillofrights.org). A brief but powerful affirmation of the right to comprehensive health services created for an LGBTQ audience by the Network of Health Equity. The Healthcare Bill of Rights can be printed out and carried in one's wallet. The website also includes information about finding inclusive care providers, contacting Lambda Legal, and filing a complaint with the DHS.

INTERSECTIONALITY, cont.

"Abortion Access for LGBTQ People," National LGBTQ Task Force (http://www.thetaskforce.org/wp-content/uploads/2016/06/TF_FactSheet_Abortion-Final.pdf). A 2016 factsheet with a focus on Texas queer and trans populations in the face of proposed drastic cuts to abortion access. Exposes sites of structural violence at the intersections of gender and sexual identity, race, and class. Affirms the core concepts of reproductive justice: "the LGBTQ and repro* movements are inseparable: we are all working for the right to live our lives with dignity and the right to choose how we use our bodies—without government intrusion."

"Lesbians and Abortions," *New York University Review of Law & Social Change*. Volume 35, No.1, p. 274, 2011. (https://papers.ssrn.com/sol3/papers.cfm?abstract_id=1822502). Academic article with a legal lens notes that "the arguments for women's freedom to be a lesbian or to have an abortion are usually articulated independently from each other" and explores how assault, identity, and stigma affect abortion access for gay women.

"Informed Consent in the Medical Care of Transgender and Gender-Non Conforming Patients," *AMA Journal of Ethics*. November 2016, Volume 18, Number 11: 1147-1155.

REPRODUCTIVE JUSTICE & ADVOCACY

The Sea Change Program (seachangeprogram.org). The Sea Change Program is a Berkeley-based initiative "dedicated to transforming the stigma around abortion and other stigmatized reproductive experiences." They are largely research-based, creating resources based on analysis of personal accounts of abortion access. Their work is written and presented accessibly and is often interactive in form.

Exhale After-Abortion Talkline (exhaleprovoice.org). Exhale has provided dedicated post-abortion support in a myriad of forms since its inception in 2000. The organization coined the term "pro-voice" to refer to a movement centering the voices of personal abortion experiences. They have partnered with media organizations such as MTV and TED to promote abortion destigmatization and illuminate the power of personal narrative.

SisterSong Women of Color Reproductive Justice Collaborative (sistersong.net). The SisterSong Women of Color Reproductive Justice Collaborative is a decentralized network of Southern health workers and advocates founded in 1997. They are the originators of the "reproductive justice" framework, illuminating the unique experiences and challenges of indigenous women and women of color. SisterSong is primarily an advocacy organization, passionately illuminating the complexity and power of women's lived experience.

We Testify (wetestify.org). The National Network of Abortion Funds' We Testify program seeks to amplify the voices of those underrepresented in abortion storytelling. We Testify is women of color-led and has intersectionality at the heart of its mission statement. We Testify is a fairly young program, but it is already taking an approach both bold and compassionate: "We testify as experts to our experiences. We testify that our spirituality and abortion are one. When we speak out and share our stories, we demand to be counted." Currently their website hosts a diverse collection of personal narratives and a small but incisive reproductive justice factsheet.

COMICS & GRAPHIC NOVELS

Abortion Eve, Lyn Chevli and Joyce Farmer, 1973. Published mere months after the Supreme Court's *Roe v. Wade* ruling in January 1973, *Abortion Eve* is an early underground comic with a positive, conversational approach to abortion access.

My Most Secret Desire, Julie Doucet, 1995. Embodiment and its discontents are often the focus of Julie Doucet's comics. In this collection, she uses dream narrative to approach her complicated relationship with sexuality and childbirth. Though most work collected is from the '90s, Doucet's neurotic, even violent approach to womanhood is still an outlier in a medium dominated by men.

Not Funny Ha-Ha, Leah Hayes, 2015. Leah Hayes' graphic novel chronicles two women's abortion experiences (one surgical, one medical) without questioning or passing judgement. Hayes does not dwell on events leading up to the abortions, instead focusing on the experience of accessing a provider and going through the abortion process. Hayes' drawings are refreshingly absent of pathos, even when expressing anxiety and discomfort.

"Medical Abortion," Oh Joy Sex Toy, Erika Moen & Matthew Nolan, 2015. (http://www.ohjoysextoy.com/medical-abortion/). A short comic about stages of pregnancy, how medical abortion works, and what to expect.

Pam Wishbow

COMICS FOR CHOICE, SECOND EDITION
ISBN 979-8-88620-014-0
First Printing, March 2023
Printed in China

Edited by Hazel Newlevant, Whit Taylor, and Ø.K. Fox
Cover illustration by Sophia Foster-Dimino
Original Book design by Jasmine Silver
Resources compiled by O Horvath

Crickx, *DLF*, and *Logisoso* fonts by Open Source Publishing (OSP)
osp.kitchen

Published by:
Silver Sprocket
1018 Valencia St, San Francisco, CA 94110, USA
www.silversprocket.net

Avi Ehrlich, Publisher
Josh PM, General Manager
Ari Yarwood, Managing Editor
Carina Taylor, Production Designer
Kyle Daileda, Publicity
Simon Jane Crowbrock, Shop Goblin
Daniel Zhou, Shop Rat
Raul Higuera-Cortez, Big Head Bandit
Sarah Maloney, Shop Cat
Sol Cintron, "Head" of "HR"
Tori Bowler, Shop Cryptid